Happiness is the Way

Want what you have, not what you don't have.

Focus on what matters

How to leverage your happiness potential to succeed sustainably.

My Holland

Cover Design by Kimberly

Cover image concept: Anthony Holland

Disclaimer

The material in this publication is of the nature of general comment only. This does not represent professional advice. To the maximum extent permitted by law, the author disclaims all responsibility and liability to any person, arising from any person taking or not taking action based on the information of this book.

ISBN: 978-0-9953550-3-3

For my parents who taught me wisdom and courage

For Anthony, My-Lan and Mai-Anh whose support and love
are infinite

Thank you for believing in me and this happy journey

Thank you Thay Thich Nhat Hanh:

"There is no way to happiness

Happiness is the way"

Summary

Are you happy? It's not a frivolous question. Most people go about their lives having all the reasons to be happy but are not. They're too busy searching for happiness, they wouldn't recognize it if it stared them right in the face. Why?

This book digs deeply into the whys and wherefores of happiness allowing us to discover remarkable insights we've taken for granted or simply ignored. The author for instance, would have us see, perhaps for the first time, that true happiness isn't about having the best of everything. It's about feeling the best of what you've got. She makes us understand (not without envy) why an average, middle income family can wake up each morning feeling like they're on top of the world, while others with fame and fortune wake up with nothing more than a lousy hangover.

Be happy. You can. This book will show you the way.

TABLE OF CONTENTS

About the Author

My was born in Villeneuve Sur Lot in France; in the south of France near Bordeaux.

She studied International Business and Japanese at Sorbonne in Paris. She completed her MBA in International Marketing in San Francisco and since then, has enjoyed the taste for cultural challenges. She has worked and lived in the USA, Japan, China, Hong Kong, Vietnam, New Zealand and now Australia. She has held a number of international business development positions. She is trained in Neuroscience, Positive Psychology, Mindfulness and Emotional Intelligence.

My specialises in creating positive change and happiness in various working environments across Australia, USA, China, Vietnam, Myanmar, New Zealand, Japan and Hong Kong. Companies and business organisations that have engaged her expertise have seen their employees transformed into a more engaged, highly motivated and more importantly, happier working group.

A certified assessor-coach and a learned lecturer, My is dedicated to bringing well-being and joy at work. She believes these do not only benefit a business but also our private relationships among family and friends, peers and associates and the community in general. For more information, check out www.equestasia.com.au.

Foreword

Some of us have *"light bulb"* moments when a new perspective arrives and our lives are instantly changed. For me it has been a gradual process of enquiry and discovery, but there was a definite eureka moment. Like many of us, I followed a fairly traditional path in both corporates and academia in various countries. As our children grew, my partner and I decided to move from the big city life in Sydney to the serenity of a small town which has provided sanctuary for people from all over the world seeking a connection with nature and genuine community values.

All this time I was looking for more meaning in my work. Then I discovered the Happiness and its Causes conference in Sydney. I knew I had found my calling. From this moment I knew my *"why"*. I knew my role was to help organisations to be better, more caring, more compassionate corporate citizens. I was deeply inspired by leading researchers in happiness and wellbeing including Barbara Fredrickson, Tal Ben-Shahar, Ed Diener, Sonja Lyubomirsky, Rick Hanson, Paul Ekman, Paul Gilbert and many others… and of course HE the Dalai Lama. These wonderful people and their deep understanding of our essential humanity changed my life and my career.

Since then I have poured my energy into studying positive psychology, neuroscience, positive neuroplasticity, mindfulness, social psychology and even magic tricks! It's wonderful to be learning and to be at the edge of knowledge, always looking forward to the latest research in emotional intelligence and the science of happiness.

I am using this knowledge to help organisations, which are struggling with unhappiness. The concept of *"happiness at work"* still challenges so many organisations, so I use the term "positive engagement", which provides a clearer link to traditional measures of corporate performance.

This book seeks to help us to understand how we can all be happier by reconnecting ourselves with the people and values that matter the most. I am very grateful for the inspiring people with whom I share this happiness journey and I hope that you will join me.

I especially hope that you are inspired to learn more about the science of happiness from the excellent thinkers and research in this field and suggest you look for signposts for your own journey in the bibliography at the end of this book.

CHAPTER 1
HAPPINESS BASICS

ONE

Introduction

"Your work is discover your world and then with all your heart give yourself to it."

Buddha

You've just heard that it's freezing cold back home, but you don't mind because you're on vacation in the tropics. In fact, right now you're floating on a raft chair in a crystal-clear swimming pool, twirling a cool drink with a festive umbrella stirrer, and taking a long sip. Are you happy?

You've been working outdoors on a hot, humid day. You're parched and perspiring. Suddenly you hear the merry tinkling of a familiar tune. It's the ice-cream man! Someone brings you a double-dip cone. It's got two scoops of your favourite flavour—and sprinkles on top. Are you happy?

Well of course you're happy! In both of these scenarios, you're experiencing highly pleasurable sensations. But what if the question went a little deeper? What if it had been, *"Are you deeply satisfied with your job and the way you work?"* or *"If you could change anything about your life, would you?"* or *"Do you believe your future is bright?"*

Ah, that's more complicated, isn't it? If you're like most of us, you'd really have to think. What exactly does it take to make you content in the present, at peace with the past, and hopeful about the future? Certainly there's nothing wrong with tropical vacations or double-dip ice-cream cones, but there's got to be more to the story.

And indeed, there is a lot more.

TWO

Pleasure or Happiness?

"The successful person is the one who finds out what is the matter with his business before his competitors do."

Roy L. Smith

Until recently, finding happiness was largely considered a personal matter. But currently the question of whether we're happy has come to be considered a pivotal issue. It has captured the attention of psychologists, economists, educators, business leaders, and health specialists.

One of the main paradoxes that these interested parties want to unravel is why, in a society where so many of us spend so much time and energy seeking pleasure and attempting to avoid pain, are so many of us depressed, anxious, pessimistic, and just plain confused? Why does enduring happiness and joy still feel so far out of reach to so many?

To begin with, there is a significant fundamental difference between happiness and pleasure. Pleasure is a fleeting feeling that comes from external circumstances: a sumptuous dinner, a relaxing massage, beautiful surroundings, and so on. Pleasure involves nice things happening to us—things that have to do with sating or

13

exciting the senses. Pleasurable experiences can certainly give us momentary positive feelings, but pleasure-based happiness does not last long—unless you try to organize all your days around pleasure, but that in itself presents other problems. Even if we could afford to chase pleasure all day, every day, the thrill of doing so would soon be gone. Our brain cells are wired to respond to novel events. After a while, repeated events or ever-present circumstances become background noise to which we barely react. This process, known as orientation and habituation, begins when we are infants and is part of the way we learn about the world. Introduce, say, a new squeeze toy to a baby and she registers intense interest and excitement (orientation) as she learns that by pressing on the toy she can elicit a fascinating noise. But after a while, the squeeze toy becomes old hat (habituation). The baby has learned all it can do, has gotten used to it, and will only be aroused by something fresh and unexpected.

All pleasurable events are subject to the same dynamics. No matter what our age, we eventually tire of things we formerly got a big kick out of. Your weeks' vacation would not be so enthralling if it went on for a year without a change in climate or venue. Your ice-cream cone would not seem so delicious if you were given one every day at the same time.

The result of habituation to pleasure is that the only way to keep it going is to raise the stakes. Sometimes this results in cravings and subsequent addiction. We become enslaved by a behaviour or a substance, such as alcohol or a narcotic, and we require more and more of the same to recreate a sensation we hope will be just like our initial rush of pleasurable feeling. (It doesn't, and so we want more yet again.) But even if we do not become addicted to something, we all too often become addicted to the mental habit of dreaming of a tomorrow where pleasure will prevail over any unpleasant feelings we have in the present. This phenomenon of continually searching for the next pleasure has been called destination addiction. We all probably know people who exemplify this dynamic behaviour. They continually promise themselves—and everyone else—that if only they can get past this problem or that obstacle and attain this or that pleasurable reward, they will finally be completely happy. But as soon as they have whatever they were wishing for, they repeat the entire if only process again. In the end, they appear to be wishing their lives away. There's no happiness in that.

None of this is to say that happiness excludes pleasure. It's not as if true happiness seekers are against vacations or ice-cream cones. (What humbugs they would be!) So you needn't worry that searching for enduring happiness means living in a secluded cave, eating rice rations, and contemplating your navel—unless, of course, that's what would give you great joy. But on a hierarchy of happiness, pleasure does not command the top slot. How could it? Anything dependent on circumstance can disappear in an instant, because circumstances are always changing. Your pleasant float in the pool chair can be interrupted when the weather turns threatening or when that cell phone you carefully tucked into your swimsuit starts to ring. Your ice-cream cone might drop to the ground or melt before you've had more than a bite.

Besides, pleasure has no profound, far-reaching consequences for your overall state of mind. In any given day, you might have more pleasant experiences than unpleasant ones, but at the end of the day it's possible that you might still be a dissatisfied, pessimistic grouch.

Pleasure, spaced at reasonable intervals so that we don't become blasé about it or addicted to it, is certainly a wonderful thing. But it would be wrong to confuse it with the kind of abiding happiness that is always accessible through all the ups and downs of life.

THREE

Money = Happiness?

*"Whenever you find yourself on the side of the
majority, it is time to pause and reflect."*

Mark Twain

If true happiness cannot be equated with moment-to-moment pleasures, can it be equated with material riches? Certainly many of us behave as if this were the case, devoting much of our lives to spending and getting, getting and spending. But the old adage that *"you can't buy happiness"* appears to be, for the most part, true.

It is true that if you are poor, a change in wealth status will certainly boost your well-being and improve your state of mind. But research shows that after achieving a certain earnings level, increased affluence does not really affect people's overall subjective sense of happiness. What's more, studies indicate that people in richer countries are not any more apt to report satisfaction with their lives than those in poorer ones. A University of Illinois study found no significant difference between the overall well-being of Fortune 500 billionaires and Massai herdsmen in eastern Africa.

In fact, too much focus on money can have an emotionally negative effect. A University of Rochester professor who studied how the desire for material wealth impacted mental health concluded that college students who put the most emphasis on affluence were prone to depression and anxiety. And jackpot lottery winners have shown that negative outcomes—including divorce, alcoholism, gambling, and loss of friends—are not uncommon when a windfall occurs.

Why doesn't being better off in material terms make us any happier? Nobel prize-winning economist Daniel Kahneman (Kahneman & Riis, 2005) says one reason is the hedonic treadmill. As our lives improve and we attain more wealth and goods that attest to our wealth—the new car, the designer wardrobe, the state-of-the-art home entertainment centre—we want even more. The luxury convertible we bought last year is nice, but not as nice as this year's model. The plasma television is great, but the next generation sets have higher resolution.

Another reason that material gain doesn't usually coincide with happiness is that we tend to compare ourselves to those who are financially better off than us, rather than to those who are not as well-off. This puts us on the social treadmill. We feel we have to keep up with, and then surpass, our neighbours, relatives, co-workers, and friends.

To feel more satisfied with your financial standing and overall happiness, compare yourself with those who are less well-off than you are. Doing so will remind you to count your blessings. It may also tempt you to spend less and avoid going into anxiety-provoking debt.

This phenomenon of constant comparison anxiety is backed up by research that shows the following:

- Many of us would choose to earn less annual income if our position relative to others improved.

- Much of our satisfaction with our income is related to the earnings of our spouse, families, or colleagues.

- Our levels of dissatisfaction go up when we perceive those around us are significantly better off than we are.

Social comparison anxiety tends to be even more aggravated in a generally well-off society where many people possess the same outward signs of status. When everyone in our neighbourhood has the same SUV in the driveway, it's hard to know where we stand. You might think this would make us calmer, but instead it makes us feel more financial stress. We wonder: what can we do, or buy, that will distinguish us as more affluent and more successful?

Some Happy Uses of Money

The good news: money's not all bad. Although prosperity so often brings with it the paradox of dissatisfaction, money can bring some satisfaction to our lives if we use it not to outdo our neighbours or satiate cravings for a surplus of material goods, but to do certain other things. Among the uses of money most likely to bring emotional fulfilment:

- **Creating and holding onto memories.** Spending money on good times—a vacation or a day out at the park—with friends and loved ones is a sound happiness investment than purchasing expensive material goods. (Although it's not a bad idea to spend a little on memory-boosters, such as photos and souvenirs.)

- **Celebrating personal accomplishments.** Going out to dinner—even a very casual one—after you finish a triathlon or after your child brings home a good report card can reinforce a sense of pride and personal accomplishment.

- **Seeing friends.** Making it a priority to spend quality time with people you like is its own reward, even if it means spending a little less time working.

- **Being more generous.** You can up your happiness quotient by earmarking some of your money for philanthropic causes. Giving to others is as beneficial to us as it is to those to whom we give. So donating money to a worthy cause is a win-win situation.

FOUR

Why Happiness Can Be Hard

"Be miserable. Or motivate yourself. Whatever has to be done, it's always your choice."

Wayne Dyer

As with all things worth achieving, however, achieving happiness is, for most of us, not necessarily a simple matter. Apart from the setbacks we often encounter in the quest to cultivate positive traits, attitudes, and behaviours, there are some genuine biological and cultural reasons why happiness can be difficult to attain and even more difficult to maintain.

Can Someone Else Make Us Happy?

It is sometimes tempting to believe that our ultimate happiness will arrive in the form of another person. A fair damsel or brave, charming prince will *"rescue"* us from any unwanted feelings and suffuse our every moment with bliss. But if that sounds like a fairy tale, it is!

Companionship is, in fact, a crucial element in achieving lasting happiness. However, to confuse the euphoric feelings of *"falling in love"*—which actually releases feel-good brain chemicals and gives us a temporary mood lift—with the lifelong satisfaction of acting lovingly is to buy into an illusion (albeit a popular, Hollywood-style illusion).

Long-term happiness does not result so much from *"falling"* in love as from *"rising"* in love. When we act in a loving way toward someone, we are ultimately more fulfilled than we are when we dwell on the fact that we are desired and admired (though that, certainly, is not a bad thing).

Acting in a loving way is not always easy. It can be quite a challenge when the people whom we love (who are, after all, only human) disagree with us, behave in ways that frustrate us, or simply have a bad day. Nevertheless, when we manage to remain kind and compassionate under trying circumstances, and when we do things that bring joy to those we love, we are more apt to achieve long-lasting personal satisfaction.

The Pursuit of Inner Happiness

The bottom line is being dependent on anything that emanates from outside of ourselves—pleasurable experiences, material goods, money, or the approval of someone else—can bring us, at most, transient positive feelings. But when we adapt to these externals, or if they are suddenly withdrawn, we then typically endure negative feelings: cravings, anxiety, perhaps even despondency.

The Fear of Happiness

Is a kind of happy-phobia possible? In some ways, it is not only possible, but also probable. At a certain level, many of us resist happiness for a number of fear-induced reasons:

- We worry that if we feel happy now we will experience a sense of let-down later—we don't let ourselves feel happy so we won't risk disappointment.

- We are afraid that if we appear happy we will draw the envy and wrath of others—and that possibly these others will go so far as to wish us or cause us harm.

- We fear looking frivolous or selfish if we are overly concerned with being happy.

- We associate happiness with a lack of intellectual acuity *("Ignorance is bliss")*.

- We feel guilty that pursuing happiness is not right or fair in a world where some people lack basic necessities.

- We don't believe we deserve to feel happy.

The fear of happiness is not to be confused with anhedonia, which is the actual inability to experience pleasure. Most people who feel irrational about happiness are able to enjoy pleasurable circumstances. They imagine, however, that if they are too happy, negative consequences will ensue.

Stuck at the Happiness Set Point?

Whatever you believe the role of evolution is in happiness, one thing is certain. Like our blood pressure and our cholesterol count, our capacity for happiness is partially determined by our genetic makeup. Researchers David Lykken and Auke Tellegen, who studied 254 sets of identical and fraternal twins, estimated that 50 percent of the traits that contribute to people's satisfaction levels are inherited. In each of us, the happiness set point, similar to a set point for body weight, is a kind of default setting to which we tend to return over and over again. Its baseline is genetically predetermined, handed down from generation to generation; happiness tends to fluctuate more or less around a predetermined happiness set point.

Things that might help us reset our happiness thermostat include the following:

- Helping others.

- Thinking as an optimist.

- Finding opportunities to laugh.

- Having close friendships and a satisfying marriage.

- Choosing work and leisure activities that engage our skills.

- Having a meaningful religious faith or spiritual practice.

- Getting enough exercise and rest.

- Meditating regularly.

Researchers continue to make great strides in determining other variables that can boost the happiness set point. Meanwhile, don't rule out the possibility that you might find something on your own that does the trick for you. Each of us can be our own experimental subject in the quest for happiness.

The Importance of Your Character

"Character is destiny," asserted Heraclitus, the ancient Greek philosopher. Our character—our innermost convictions, values, and virtues—plays an essential part in determining how happy we will be throughout our lifetime. For a long time psychology steered clear of studying character. The subject had a moral connotation that many felt was an inappropriate focus for science. But such is no longer the case. As this chapter shows, it is virtually impossible to understand happiness without considering what character is,

how it is formed, and why it has the potential to drive our most positive actions.

The Happiness-Character Link

The components of character are known as character strengths. The more strengths we have, and the greater their potency, the better able we will be not only to appreciate happiness but to actively choose and create it— even in difficult circumstances.

But even people who may never have consciously considered exactly what good character consists of tend to recognize it when they see it. As the following example shows, you don't need to be a psychologist to appreciate the powerful way in which character can shape an individual's response to life events.

Quite a Character: One Man's Example

In the fall of 2007, Randy Pausch (Pausch), a Carnegie Mellon University computer-science professor, gave what was billed as his *"last lecture"* to 400 students and colleagues. The *"last lecture"* is a popular title for talks on college campuses in which top professors give hypothetical "final" talks about the things that matter most to them. The difference in this situation was that Pausch, a 46-year-old father of three, had been diagnosed with terminal pancreatic cancer. He was literally, not figuratively, imparting his final words of wisdom to his audience. The professor began his talk by showing CT scans of the tumours that would prematurely end his life within a few months. He then announced that if anyone expected him to be *"morose,"* he was sorry to disappoint them. On the heels of that statement he gleefully segued into a series of one-handed um.

During the lecture that followed his display of physical prowess, Pausch talked about his very specific childhood dreams—to walk in zero gravity, to write a World Book Encyclopaedia entry, to design Disney rides, and to win enormous stuffed animals whenever carnivals came to town. He noted that he had achieved each and every goal—and then distributed his stuffed animal cache among audience members, saying he would not need them anymore. In another section of his talk, Pausch flashed across a screen a series of rejection letters he'd been sent in the course of his career. Obviously relishing his setbacks, he told his listeners that *"Brick walls are there for a reason. They let us prove how badly we want things."*

Pausch advised his listeners to be patient: *"Wait long enough, and people will surprise and impress you."* He encouraged creativity: after showing photos of his childhood bedroom, decorated with math notations he'd scrawled on the walls, he said, *"If your kids want to paint their bedrooms, as a favour to me, let 'em do it."* He espoused the joys of altruism: *"Helping others fulfil their dreams is even more fun than achieving your own."*

Pausch talked about his legacy, saying he would *"live on in Alice,"* a Carnegie Mellon software project he helped create that allows users to create 3-D animations. He paid homage to his parents, who'd let him write on his walls; brought out a birthday cake for his wife, whose birthday had been the day before; and noted that he was having the talk videotaped so that his children, ages 5, 2, and 1, could watch it when they were older.

After the professor's speech, the audience rose for an ovation. They were applauding more than the talk, however. They were applauding a life well-lived—a life filled with pleasure, meaning, and purpose. In a sense they were applauding the unfolding of one man's exemplary character.

How Character Carries Us Through

Randy Pausch might be defined as a paragon of good character. His final message strikingly summed up a lifetime of attitudes and actions that enabled him not only to achieve his dreams but to manifest resilience in the face of defeat and even death. What are the elements that made Pausch a man of strong, virtuous character, and, by extension, a happy man? Among the qualities he displayed were:

- The imagination and creativity to envision unique and complex goals

- The perseverance and determination to pursue these goals

- Zest and enthusiasm for life's pleasures

- A love of learning

- Self-motivation

- Gratitude for the entirety of his life experience

- Love for his family

- Respect for his students and colleagues

- A spirit of giving

- A sense of humour and whimsy

- Courage

- A sense of optimism and perspective

From Pausch's stories it appears that many of these traits were constant influences in both his personal and professional life. Some, like his creativity, love of learning, and self-motivation, were evident even in boyhood. But how might Pausch's character have developed? For that matter, how does character develop in any of us? Are we simply born with character?

Temperament, Personality, and Character

Social scientists studying character contend that any character strength may have its prodigies—precocious children or adolescents who display the trait early and naturally. But positive psychologists do not assume that character traits are fixed or grounded in an immutable genetic code.

In other words, we're not born with character. We are born with a bundle of predispositions known as temperament. As babies we are more than blank slates.

Is Personality the Same as Character?

In the months after birth, early manifestations of temperament are already subject to change. The changes occur as babies interact with their caregivers. Parents' reactions to their child's style of behaviour can strengthen it or weaken it. For example, parents can react to a *"difficult"* child by becoming more rigid about scheduling and less responsive to outbursts. But this in turn can make the infant even more difficult to handle. On the other hand, parents can respond in ways that nudge temperament in a more positive direction—perhaps by becoming more adaptable themselves, or by reframing a child's boisterous cry as a sign of hardiness rather than an accusatory commentary on their parenting skills. (That kid's got some pair of lungs. What a ball of energy!) Parents' response to their infant's temperament is only the first of countless environmental factors that will contribute to an individual's overall personality. Soon the child will be influenced by peers, teachers, neighbours, the media, and the sum total of cultural messages. The adult personality that develops over ensuing years is a complex overlay of behavioural patterns and attitudes, emotional reactions, and social roles.

As personality develops, character is also formed and also influenced by these multiple and overlapping factors. But personality and character are not the same things. The first is overt, the latter internal. Put another way: when we interact with anyone, personality is what we see; character is what we get.

Characteristics of Character Strength

It's possible to spend 10 minutes in a casual exchange with someone and come away with a fairly strong sense of his or her personality traits. We might describe that person as shy or outgoing, serious or merry, forceful or laid back. However, it usually takes far longer to assess someone's character. We don't know if they are brave or loyal or compassionate until we see them put to some sort of test and have to choose between courses of action. As Aristotle pointed out, when we speak of an excellence of character, the emphasis is not on mere distinctiveness or individuality, but on the combination of qualities that people find admirable.

Character is complex. It involves the interplay of many traits and many influences. But there are some constants.

Good Character Takes Work

Everyone develops a personality, and everyone develops character. But to develop the sort of character that can generate happiness is not a passive act. It requires conscious choice and volition. In other words, we have to work at it. As positive psychology movement founder Martin Seligman (Seligman, 2004) has pointed out, there are many shortcuts to pleasure, from drugs to casual sex to TV to shopping, but there are no shortcuts to the good life that is derived from character strengths. Indeed, to make life decisions based on character-linked convictions can often seem like anything but the easy way out. Traits such as self-control, loyalty, and humility can sometimes get in the way of, say, turning a quick (albeit unethical) profit or indulging in an illicit love affair. But in the end, an individual can derive more satisfaction from habits that derive from good character than from giving in to impulses to quench an immediate desire.

Character Is Values-Based

What makes character strengths a matter of conscious choice is that they are based on values? Life's important decisions involve choosing from among a variety of options. When we select goals we consider worthy, we are acting out of a sense of personal values. For example, if we value knowledge, we may decide to spend our time reading books, attending seminars, or pursuing an advanced degree. If we value the love of family, we may decide to arrange our life to encompass more family time. If we value kindness, we will be aware of how we speak to people, even when we are angry.

Everyone has beliefs about what is valuable to them, so everyone has values. And most people are aware of the sorts of virtuous values that their culture, society, and spiritual traditions hold dear. The values prescribed by spiritual traditions throughout the world and throughout time are strikingly similar. So presumably everyone has an idea of what options he or she should pursue to embody good character and reap the rewards of doing so. But whether they do so—and to what degree—is another matter.

Ideal values are not always easy to achieve; even if you value honesty highly, try being totally honest with everyone you meet for 24 hours and you will understand the challenge. Understandably, many people find it easier to articulate admirable values than to actually practice them. And virtually everyone at some time or other will need to make some compromises between, say, self-interest and self-sacrifice, or between calculation and compassion. Still, some people's words match their deeds more often than other people's. In the end, exhibiting the kind of character that generates happiness involves not simply talking the talk but actually walking the walk. Character strengths can be considered values on which action is taken with some degree of consistency, even—or especially—in times when circumstances are trying and the proverbial chips are down. As Napoleon said, *"To have the right estimate of a man's character, we must see him in adversity."*

Emotions Pass, Character Lasts

Even people who are arguably of sterling character and who frequently put their strengths into practice are perfectly capable of experiencing emotions that run counter to the behavioural choices they see as more valuable and productive. However, one thing such individuals appear to understand is that emotions pass, while character lasts. Often, they can feel like behaving badly and still do what will, in the end, produce a more positive outcome. They may feel angry, but still behave kindly—most of the time. They may feel lazy, but still behave industriously—most of the time.

As for those situations when their behaviour does not follow their beliefs, these individuals do not forsake their values and strengths afterward but use them as a home base they can return to. Their character strengths anchor them even after a rush of powerful emotion may succeed in temporarily derailing them. Some social scientists say character is a mere matter of situationism, and that any of us will sacrifice our character strengths under certain combinations of circumstances, such as when fear of authority causes us to follow questionable orders. But positive psychologists contend this is a simplistic way of looking at character. Even if they do stray, fundamentally happy people do not consider a character transgression an excuse to surrender their usual virtues any more than successful dieters consider an occasional ice-cream cone a reason to give up their weight-loss plan.

Character Can Be Improved

Is character malleable or fixed? With neurobiologists searching for brain-linked causes or contributors to virtually every human behaviour, it's not surprising that they are also currently looking for neurochemical forces that drive our impulses to do good or do wrong. At the University of Zurich, for example, researchers relate a person's level of trust to a measure of their neuropeptide levels. They also relate an individual's level of fairness to the electromagnetic pattern in their right prefrontal cortex—and have noted that if you disrupt that pattern with a strong magnet, a person's sense of fair play will be snuffed out like a match flame in a brisk wind.

However, additional research has yielded far fuzzier results on how the brain makes values-based decisions. Ask an individual a series of increasing knotty ethical questions, and with each escalating layer of complication, more and more regions of the brain become active—presumably doing battle while the individual ponders a course of action. It appears that values-based actions are a holistic affair, with many cognitive and emotional *"moving parts"* factoring in.

Where Does Character Come From?

Humans are social creatures, and our character dispositions have a significant social learning component. Whether we are aware of it or not, the values that inform our character are, in part, shaped and moulded by influential people around us and by institutions in whose circle of influence we fall.

Moms, Dads, Models, and Morals

Our species is skilled at imitation. Humans are born mimics, naturally imitating the people around us as we develop. Developmental psychologists have long observed that as we grow we absorb and recreate not only the actions of those around us but also their attitudes and values. We *"read"* what those close to us are thinking and notice how they are deliberating when faced with a challenge or dilemma. We hear what they say, and—more importantly—we observe what they do. This is known as modelling. We use these people as role models-templates on which to pattern our own values-based behaviours.

Not surprisingly, the people in our immediate families—most notably our parents—are our first role models of character and instructors of values. They may or may not sit us down and say, *"Let me tell you about courage,"* or *"Here's what I know about the rewards of persistence,"* but we observe the decisions they make and the values those decisions embody, and we learn what their hopes and expectations are for our own behaviour.

In addition to modelling, parents can also influence our values by behavioural means, by doling out rewards and punishments. Through this type of reinforcement, we learn that acting on the values our parents consider positive will get us something positive. Acting in opposition to those values, on the other hand, will yield unpleasant consequences.

Finally, parents are early gatekeepers of our worldly information. The books and films and television shows they expose us to when we are small are also filled with ideas, behaviours, role models, and values-based lessons. Thus, The Little Engine That Could teaches us about perseverance, Asian of The Chronicles of Narnia teaches us about bravery, and The Simpsons teaches us that a sense of humour is important, too.

Influential Institutions

As we move out into the wider world, we encounter institutions and organizations that impart values-based lessons in a cognitive way. Many children attend some form of religious instruction classes that fulfil this role. Many belong to groups such as Boy Scouts, whose values lessons can be summed up in the Boy Scout law, which stipulates that a Scout is *"loyal, helpful, friendly, courteous, kind, obedient, cheerful, thrifty, brave, clean, and reverent."*

Schools, those ubiquitous institutions in which young people spend so much of their time, have always been influential in shaping values, whether they acknowledge this or not. Today, however, many schools formalise this role by implementing character education programs. These programs systematise values-driven lessons, attempt to create an environment where the school itself functions in accordance with those values, and often recognise students for displaying character traits that are consistent with those values, such as responsibility, self-control, fairness, tolerance, and consideration of others. Organisations and institutions can certainly play a part in forming our values and in creating character strengths. However, they are most effective when the lessons they impart and the virtues they endorse resonate with those taught at home.

The Self-Examination Factor

At any juncture in our life from childhood on, we may face a challenging situation that compels us to look within and ask ourselves, *"What is the right thing to do?"* As we make such choices over and over—with *"no one watching,"* as it were—we can actually map the landscape of our own virtues.

As far as the psychology of happiness is concerned, character strengths are always capable of evolving. We are always capable of discovering a new strength, of resurrecting a dormant strength, or of enhancing a strength we use routinely. Life will be our instructor if we let it be. And the more we let life instruct us, the happier that life will turn out to be.

FIVE

Character Strengths

"Don't be afraid to give up the good to go for the great."

John D. Rockefeller

If someone were to ask you about your character strengths, you might not know how to answer. It's possible you never thought about yourself in those terms. If you did answer, you might say something general, such as *"I'm a nice person"* or *"I have integrity."* But each and every one of us has specific strengths and virtues we can draw upon to promote happiness. Identifying them is the first step to making the most of them. This chapter looks at what constitutes happiness-enhancing strengths, as well as how we can recognize and build upon our own.

Areas of Character Strength

Positive psychologists have considered, and are still considering at great length, exactly, which aspects of character can help us live a life that is not only enjoyable but also filled with meaning and purpose. Dr. Martin Seligman and Dr. Chris Peterson (Peterson & Seligman, Character strengths and virtues: A handbook and classification, 2004), along with other top scholars in the country, spearheaded the research to create the extensive Values in Action (VTA) classification, which defines six general categories of overriding virtues—wisdom, courage, justice, humanity, temperance, and spirituality. They then defined the paths by which each of these virtues is expressed, resulting in 24 character strengths.

Other positive psychologists have grouped strengths somewhat differently. For example, Dr. Stephen Post, professor of bioethics at Case Western University and president of the institute for Research on Unlimited Love, conceives of character strengths in 10 major rubrics: celebration, generativity, forgiveness, courage, humour, respect, compassion, loyally, listening, and creativity.

Yet the essence of the strengths and virtues remains the same, regardless of which listing or categorization one consults. Strengths link to values and virtue, and all require expending positive effort via our minds, hearts, and spirits. They relate to how we treat ourselves, how we treat others, and how we relate to the human condition at large.

The summary of strengths that follows is an encapsulation of those most frequently cited, grouped into categories of cognitive strengths, goal-oriented strengths, self-mastery strengths, interpersonal strengths, and transcendent strengths.

Cognitive Strengths

Cognitive strengths are strengths of mental focus. They spring from valuing knowledge. Individuals who display these strengths are interested in accumulating knowledge not just for their own sakes but also because of what that knowledge may enable them to do. Among the focus-oriented strengths positive psychologists most often cite are creativity, curiosity, reason, and social and emotional intelligence:

- Creativity involves inventiveness and imagination—the ability to generate ideas, artefacts, and solutions to problems that are both novel and useful.

- Curiosity involves the love of learning and an eagerness to discover more about a wide range of things, including people, places, ideas, and natural phenomena.

- Reason involves the ability to think critically and logically, to make sound decisions with regard to one's self and others without being unduly swayed by fleeting emotions.

- Social and emotional intelligence involves knowledge of one's own intrapsychic workings and knowledge of the most effective means of relating positively to other people.

Creativity can contribute to happiness in myriad ways. To actively be in a creative state is to be highly energized and attentive to the process at hand—so engaged that time flies, and everyday worries and mundane concerns seem to vanish for the duration. But creativity does more than temporarily distract people from their problems. Creative people think in flexible and divergent ways that can actually help them resolve their problems and meet life's challenges. Curiosity connotes openness to new experiences. Curious people continually want to know more about various aspects of the world around them, about others, or about themselves. They are never bored or apathetic, because there is always something more to understand and appreciate. Not surprisingly, curiosity correlates highly with physical health and longevity, probably because curious people always want to know what tomorrow will bring and are curious about matters pertaining to their own well-being.

Reason can contribute to life satisfaction by orienting us toward reality and positive ways to cope with and adapt to it. Emotional and social intelligence helps us negotiate the complex landscape of emotions and interpersonal relationships in thoughtful, constructive ways.

Goal-Oriented Strengths

Goal-oriented strengths are related to accomplishment. They spring from the values of achievement and determination. People with goal-oriented strengths are self-motivators. They are proactive rather than reactive. Perseverance, courage, and conscientiousness are among the key strengths in this category:

- Courage comes in many forms; it can involve taking great risks and changing the world, but it can also involve the everyday heroism needed to face a new day in spite of hardships and difficulties.

- Perseverance involves making a commitment—to an ideal, to a course of action, to a relationship—and holding fast to that commitment in spite of challenges.

- Conscientiousness encompasses thoroughness and diligence in performing tasks.

Courage, persistence, and conscientiousness can help individuals become successful in whatever they pursue. But even when worldly success per se is elusive, these strengths can uplift the spirits and increase pride and self-respect. The brave are also often very influential people. Their courage inspires others, which in turn makes the courageous feel gratified. People rich in goal-oriented strengths are adept at finding meaning and articulating their purpose in life. They know what they want to do and are brave and dedicated enough to do whatever it takes.

Self-Mastery Strengths

Strengths of self-mastery are, in essence, traits of self-discipline and balance. They relate to the value of self-control. They require the ability to refrain from impulsivity and overindulgence. Typical self-mastery strengths include moderation and modesty:

- Moderation involves resisting the temptation to give in to recklessness, destructive excess, or deprivation in any and all activities, even in one's attitudes.

- Modesty means being humble enough to know that one cannot know all, do all, or have all.

Moderation is the art of controlling cravings, addictions, and unreasonable desires that can prove excessive or harmful. And almost anything can prove harmful in extremes. Having a goal and working toward it, for example, can lead to happiness. But obsessively working toward that goal to the exclusion of fulfilling relationships and personal health will lead to a lack of balance and perspective.

Modesty is itself a kind of moderation—a moderation of grandiosity and boastfulness. It is true that happy people have high self-regard, but those with inflated egos and arrogant attitudes are not displaying healthy self-esteem but actually indicating a deficit in their self-image. Those who possess modesty and humility are more open-minded, more flexible, and more accessible to other people.

Interpersonal Strengths

Other-oriented strengths relate to the values of compassion, cooperation, and basic regard for others with whom we share our lives and the planet. The strengths include kindness, fairness, empathy, generosity, trust, loyalty, forgiveness, and genuineness:

- Kindness involves treating people with universal goodwill, as we ourselves would wish to be treated.

- Fairness involves open-mindedness and a respect for equity and justice for all.

- Empathy is the ability to understand other people's points of view, to listen to them nonjudgmentally, and to experience the world through their eyes.

- Altruism involves a spirit of generosity, a willingness to share one's resources —not only wealth but time, effort, and spirit—with others.

- Trust means displaying an optimistic view of human nature that gives people the benefit of the doubt.

- Loyalty involves the ability to make enduring commitments to those we love and respect.

- Forgiveness involves the ability to stop dwelling on hurts, to put the past behind and move forward.

- Genuineness encompasses openness, authenticity, honesty, and receptivity to others.

A lot of interpersonal strengths contribute to forging strong, close, supportive relationships. Research overwhelmingly shows that strong relationships on the individual and community level are direct instigators of happiness. The same is true of altruistic behaviour.

Transcendent Strengths

Transcendent strengths allow us to rise above negative circumstances. They enable us to weather the ups and downs of daily life with greater peace and equanimity, and— on occasion—to surpass what we may have thought of as our limits. Transcendent strengths include hope, reverence, gratitude, enthusiasm, and humour:

- Hope involves an optimistic spirit, a belief that the best can come to pass, and that whatever happens, faith may be for the best even if we don't understand why at the time. Reverence means allowing oneself to enter a state of awe, amazement, wonder, and deep appreciation—it has a spiritual component even if not tied to a formal religious faith.

- Gratitude involves the active expression of thankfulness for the positive things in one's life.

- Enthusiasm means embracing life, going forth into the world each day with a joyous anticipation and a tendency to say *"yes."*

- Humour was aptly defined by comedian Mel Brooks as *"a defence against the universe"*—it allows us to dispel frustration, counter stress, and reframe experience in a more positive way.

Transcendent strengths are tied to what psychologists in the human potential movement called self-actualization. People strong in transcendent qualities tend to value the ideal of reaching their highest potential. That noble quest itself can be a source of immense contentment.

Evaluating Your Strengths

Look down any list of character strengths and some will probably resonate or ring a bell. You might have shocks of recognition and think, *"that describes me exactly,"* or *"I'm like that—at least sometimes."* That's a good start toward identifying your strengths.

But which strengths would you say are your trademark strengths? Which ones do you tend to use repeatedly and effectively to enhance your life? Which ones have you drawn on when the going got tough?

Identifying these can be invaluable. When you know what strengths define you, you can consciously build on them to boost your overall happiness.

Recall When Strengths Saved You

Did you ever use your social intelligence and sense of humour to deflect the menace of a schoolyard bully? Did you ever use your creativity to improvise your way through a presentation at work when your projector failed and your PowerPoint slides proved useless? Have you ever been told you could not possibly achieve something and still found it within yourself to persevere and prevail? Have you ever faced a dire personal situation—perhaps a serious illness or loss—where your courage and hope sustain you?

Try recalling and then writing down stories in your life that involve such situations. It doesn't matter how old you were, and the outcome needn't have changed the world—it need only have made your personal experience richer and more gratifying.

Write Yourself a Letter of Recommendation

Another way to identify your strengths is to take a third-party perspective. Step back and try to view yourself through the eyes of those whom you've most impressed in your life: teachers, coaches, co-workers, bosses, parents, spouses, or even your own children. Now write a letter as if it were coming from one of the people that hold you in high regard. How would they recommend you for a job, a promotion, a college acceptance, or even a blind date?

Seeing your strengths in writing can be a satisfying experience in itself. But when you have your list you'll want to review it periodically. Doing so will give you a chance to add to it, amend it, and note which skills you employ most often. Remember especially to consult your list in times of difficulty or when you need ideas and inspiration. The list will remind you of all the tools you have in your tool belt.

Skills and Talents

In addition to character strengths, each of us possesses specific talents and abilities that can also contribute to our happiness. We tend to experience pleasure and a sense of meaning and purpose when we are actively using our talents.

Our skills and talents often tie in to something termed multiple intelligences. For example, an individual may have talents in one or a number of realms. Athletic skills involve grace, dexterity, stamina, and *"muscle memory,"* or recalling things through one's body rather than verbally or visually. Athletic and body movement abilities can translate into being good at anything from basketball to boxing to ballet.

Linguistic skills involve anything related to language, including a facility with reading, writing, and persuasive speaking. People with language abilities may excel in anything (or everything) from doing crossword puzzles to writing poetry to debating to teaching. They are also likely to have excellent memories for information they hear and read.

Math and logic skills have to do with numbers, patterns and sequence recognition, abstractions, and inductive and deductive reasoning. Those who have talent in this area are often good at complex calculations and scientific investigation.

People with spatial and visual skills are good at envisioning how things will look and how they will fit together. They are good at manipulating objects. Their visual memory is strong and they have a good sense of location and direction. They may be artistically inclined or have a strong aptitude for engineering.

Musical skills relate to sound, rhythm, pitch, and all aspects of music. People with such abilities may be good at singing, at playing instruments, and at composing. They also have excellent audio memory.

Naturalistic skills involve relating well to one's natural surroundings. People with these skills have an exceptional sensitivity to nature. They may be good at growing and gardening, at analysing climates and environments, and even at relating to animals.

Unlike character strengths, which take effort and will to enact, our talents may seem to come naturally to us. We might feel we have a *"knack"* or even a *"gift"* for certain activities. But we are usually most happy when we are not only using our skills but also honing them and stretching them.

Building and Renewing Strengths and Skills

Not everyone possesses every talent or character strength. Skills and strengths can certainly be acquired, but one sure-fire path to unhappiness is to sit around pining about what you don't have. If you want to cultivate a skill or strength, by all means do so! But one of the best paths to happiness is to build on the skills and strengths you already possess. Dust off dormant skills and strengths and take them to new heights. Think of ways you can merge and use them together. And whenever you can, use a strength or skill in a new way. This combines the pleasure of novelty with the satisfaction of purpose.

Suppose, for example, you have a talent for language and a strong sense of fairness and justice. Find a compelling issue and start a *"letter to the editor"* campaign to speak out for the underprivileged. Suppose you are creative and funny. Think about taking the stage for *"open mike"* night at your local comedy club. (This ought to brush up your courage as well!) Suppose you have athletic agility and a tremendous amount of perseverance. Are you up for running a marathon?

These are just a few of myriad possibilities. The idea is to maximize your existing potential to make yourself happier. Life will never feel stale to those who take this approach.

CHAPTER 2
HELPING OTHERS

SIX

The Importance of Altruism

"Love only grows by sharing. You can only have more for yourself by giving it away to others."

Brian Tracy

Imagine you wanted to take a crash-course in character instruction. If you asked your instructor for one guiding rule or principle by which to live with pleasure, meaning, and purpose, he would probably cite some version of what we know as the Golden Rule:

"Do unto others as you would have others do unto you."

As it turns out, this principle is not only the Golden Rule of morality and spirituality, but also a path to cultivating a high level of personal happiness. By living altruistically, we can make the most of all our best character traits by using them to benefit others.

The Altruism Urge

Acts of compassion, generosity, and everyday kindness all fall under the collective heading of altruism. The word altruism comes from the Latin word alter, meaning "other," and refers to helping others. But altruism generates a high rate of return for those who bestow it as well as those who receive it. Altruism is a phenomenon as ancient as humankind itself. Some researchers believe that altruism played a role in the development of the human race, because our ancestors gained evolutionary advantages by helping one another to hunt, gather food, and defend against predators. Altruism probably contributed to the development of many other kinds of positive social behaviour, such as sharing, communication, and laughter.

"I do not know what your destiny is, but I know this. Those who seek and find ways to help others will find true happiness." —Dr. Albert Schweitzer

If we hear someone contend that altruism is a universal part of human nature, however, we might be prone to scepticism. It's sometimes all too easy to think of individuals whose blatantly selfish actions seem to embody the opposite of altruism: ruthless dictators, hardened criminals, con artists, and terrorists. But consider two things: first, those people who are decidedly non-altruistic don't seem very happy, do they? Second, as with any so-called universal trait, there is always variation among individuals. Our species thrives on altruism, but some of us are more prone to altruism than others.

Still, all humans have within us the capacity to be altruistic. Moreover, we can expand our altruistic actions if we consciously choose to do so. Why would we choose to do this? The answer is something of a paradox. Although altruism is defined as a form of selflessness, it is actually a form of enlightened self-interest. When we help someone, they get something and we get something. With altruism, everyone's a winner.

"Every man must decide whether he will walk in the light of creative altruism or in the darkness of destructive selfishness."—Martin Luther King Jr.

SEVEN

Do Good, Feel Good

"You can make more friends in two months by becoming interested in other people than you can in two years by trying to get other people interested in you."

Dale Carnegie

A common assignment to students who take courses in psychology is to indulge in an activity that provides pure sensory pleasure and then engage in an activity that involves helping someone else. On completing the assignment, many students are amazed to find that they felt appreciably happier after helping someone else (for example, tutoring a fellow student, volunteering at a soup kitchen or animal shelter, or shovelling snow for a neighbour) than they did after engaging in pure pleasure (for example, eating a sumptuous meal, attending a concert, or making love on the beach).

Research backs up what those students have discovered on a personal level. It consistently shows that when we act with kindness and compassion on behalf of other people, we experience a sense of emotional well-being and comfort as well as a diminished sense of stress.

How does this work? Altruism stimulates the brain's positive emotion centres. Using MRI scans, scientists have noted that regions of the brain associated with generating positive emotion are highly active when we experience empathetic and compassionate emotions.

Helpful behaviour also triggers feel-good hormones. The brain's pleasure-linked chemicals, such as dopamine and various endorphins are released into the bloodstream when we engage in helpful behaviour. These hormones can create a burst of euphoric energy, a so-called helper's high.

A recent study has identified high levels of the hormone oxytocin in people who are being generous toward others. Oxytocin is connected to an adaptive positive response to stress known as *"tend and befriend."* An alternative to the *"fight or flight"* response, which can create edginess and aggression, *"tend and befriend"* prompts us to manage stress by affiliating with others and working cooperatively. Oxytocin is best known for its role in preparing mothers for motherhood, but the hormone is present in both men and women, and spikes when a member of either gender lends a helping hand.

The term helper's high was coined in 1988 by researcher Allen Luks, on noting that 50 percent of those who helped others reported feeling "high" when doing so. Forty-three percent felt stronger and more energetic.

Helping behaviour alleviates depression across the life cycle. Various studies have shown that giving and generosity reduce teen depression and that teens who are giving are happier than their less-altruistic peers. Additional research has shown that the same holds true at the other end of the life cycle. A study conducted by sociologists at the University of Texas at Austin found that volunteering substantially reduces symptoms of depression for adults older than age 65.

Helping others raises our self-esteem and enables us to forgive our own mistakes. A study of older Americans revealed that those who lent emotional support to others demonstrated an increased willingness to forgive themselves for their own failings and shortcomings. This self-forgiveness is key to a sense of well-being.

Altruism not only puts us in a happier state, but also enables us to remain in that state for a longer stretch of time. Researchers conducting longitudinal studies—the sort that follows subjects for decades, interviewing them extensively at various intervals—have concluded that people who are givers suffer fewer stress-created illnesses and add years to their life span.

EIGHT

Active Altruism

"I believe that in this new world that we live in, we often have a responsibility, you know, to actually go beyond the thou shalt nots - that is, the not harming others - and say we can help others and we should be helping others."

Peter Singer

Not surprisingly, those who demonstrate altruistic behaviour early in life tend to keep on doing so. Without doubt their behaviour brings them a great deal of gratification and this positive reinforcement keeps them behaving in a helpful, generous way.

But not everyone practices helping his or her neighbours—or anyone else—at an early age. Those who have positive role models in their families or are involved in community-based or faith-based organisations that stress service are usually more likely to make helping a habit than those who lack such affiliations. The good news, of course, is that it is never too late to catch up. There are many ways to make contributions, both large and small, to the well-being of others.

Looking Within Your Community

Who would benefit from your help? Who would appreciate some generosity and kindness? The first place it might seem natural to look is in your immediate surroundings. You can get some ideas by simply walking down your street. There are your elderly neighbours. Could they use help with their errands—or could they just use some friendly company? There's the local elementary school. Perhaps you can do something for the students—or the teachers. There's the local park—could it do with a clean-up?

If you are hesitant to jump in on your own, don't worry. An abundance of volunteer organizations can help you figure out how to give some of your time on a regular basis. And joining a group will also add to your happiness because you will have the added satisfaction of meeting like-minded people, sharing ideas, and pitching in to achieve a goal you might not have been able to achieve on your own.

To find an opportunity that is right for you, first consider your talents and strengths. People are happy when they are doing what they're good at—and volunteering is no exception. If you have a way with animals, that SPCA dog-walking position might be right up your alley. If you're a natural mentor type, Big Brothers or Big Sisters can be your perfect match. If carpentry is your thing, consider Habitat for

Humanity—an organization that builds houses for the underprivileged and for disaster victims.

Not enough time to volunteer? Many of the busiest and most successful people do so. In the end it will buy you more time. Two large studies found that volunteers live longer than non-volunteers. And one of those found a 44 percent reduction in early death rates among adults who volunteered on a regular basis. That effect on longevity is greater than that of exercising four times a week. Consider your values, too. What is important to you in terms of what is happening in your community? Are you concerned about the environment? Look for an organization that works to preserve, protect, or restore natural habitats. Are you concerned about education? Consider tutoring or homework help opportunities, or consider Literacy Volunteers. Are you interested in furthering public health? Look for service opportunities at local hospitals or at organizations that conduct blood drives, free clinics, and the like.

Consider the level of personal contact you're comfortable with. It can be somewhat gratifying to do the kind of volunteering that is "once-removed," such as collecting clothes for the Salvation Army or books for library drives. But many people find that volunteering is ultimately more satisfying if they meet and spend time with the people they are helping. The same holds true if you enjoy working with animals. Selling raffles so the local shelter can care for more cats is great, but it will most likely be even more happiness-inducing if you are at least occasionally able to stroke and snuggle some real-live kittens.

What level of commitment are you looking for? Many organizations need volunteers solely in response to a particular problem or situation (such as in the aftermath of a hurricane or earthquake). Other organizations have seasonal needs for helpers (perhaps to distribute food or gifts to needy families at holiday time). These are worthy causes and no one should hesitate to pitch in. But beyond this, it is a good idea for happiness-seekers to integrate volunteering into their schedule on a regular weekly basis. This way the benefits of giving will remain a steady factor in your emotional well-being. If no perfect-fit volunteer groups immediately come to mind, you can easily find a local non-profit group that needs your help by simply looking in your local telephone book. You can also conduct a very specific Internet search. If you belong to a church, mosque, or temple, that is a wonderful place to inquire about helping opportunities in the general community.

You might wish to consider devoting some of your vacation time to a "volunteer vacation," which is an increasingly popular way of spending one's leisure time both pleasurably and purposefully.

Spontaneous Altruism

Some people are reluctant to help others because they are preoccupied with their own problems. Yet after you start to help others, you will find that your preoccupation with your own problems recedes, and with it the anxiety that can block your happiness. This can be especially true when you stay open to the possibility of helping others in the moment as opportunity presents itself. If you cultivate an attitude of alertness to what others need, you will be less prone to self-absorbed worry and rumination. You will be broadening your perspective and opening up your inner world.

Naturally you may find lots of opportunities to offer in-the-moment assistance to members of your immediate family and circle of friends. Providing such help is part of the implicit bargain we make in family life and friendships: you help me and I'll help you. Your helpfulness, in such instances, will contribute to your loved ones' well-being and to yours, because your needs mutually impact one another. *Quid pro quo*.

We are most likely to help others when we are feeling happy and secure. This well-documented phenomenon is known as the "feel good, do good" effect. But don't rule out helping out when your mood is less than great. It's good medicine for the blues, because helping can be an instant mood booster.

But let's take it one step further. What if you make it a point to remain alert to opportunities to perform some sort of altruistic act for casual acquaintances or even for complete strangers whom you most likely will never see again: the driver who needs a break getting into your lane in traffic, the shopper laden down with too many grocery bags, the novice exerciser at the gym who needs a word of encouragement? How would that make you happy? Here's what's in it for you:

- *An expanded sense of community.* Isolation and loneliness can result from our feeling that we are "separate" from everyone else. Keeping an eye out for one another reinforces the idea that, although we are all unique individuals, we are all connected. To help one is to help all, including yourself.

- *A "helper's high."* Pitching in where you can and making yourself universally useful increases your chances of achieving a helper's high on a routine basis. A random act of kindness can release your endorphins and stimulate the positive emotion centres in your brain.

- A contagious smile. When you help a stranger, your immediate *"payment"* is often a smile of acknowledgement and gratitude. A smile is something we can easily *"catch"* from someone else. It's infectious. Someone smiles at us and we smile back without even thinking about it. The mere physical act of smiling enhances our mood.

- A diminished stress level. The physiological sensations that occur within us when we help can counter our level of negative stress. Being ready, willing, and able to help acquaintances and strangers throughout the day can be an ongoing strategy for keeping stress in check.

- Moral or spiritual satisfaction. The obligation to help others is a basic tenet of virtually every faith and of any service organization. Acts of spontaneous kindness can help us feel more in tune with such uplifting positive teachings.

Helping at random requires an attitude of empathy and compassion, and a willingness to keep at least part of your focus on something other than yourself. The Boy Scouts exhort their members to *do a good deed daily.* Judaism reminds its followers to perform a daily mitzvah, or good turn. Buddhism reminds its followers of the principle of karma, a law of cause and effect that implies our positive intent resonates universally and, eventually, returns to us in some form. And Christianity teaches that we reap what we sow.

But fear not: there are no needs to give up your worldly possessions, quit your job, and wander the earth helping needy souls. It is perfectly possible to change nothing about your life except to open your eyes to opportunities to be kind and still raise your happiness quotient substantially. Moreover, most spontaneous helping does not necessitate devoting your entire day, or even a substantial fraction of it. It takes only moments to pay a compliment, laugh at someone's joke, hold a door open, or wave someone ahead of you in the supermarket express line.

NINE

OVERHELPING

*"We have so far to go to realize our human potential
for compassion, altruism, and love."*

Jane Goodall

Though the happiness engendered in helping others is clear, anything can be taken to drastic extremes and thus become unhealthy. Helping others will not help you, or them, if you deprive and neglect your own needs—or if you do things that diminish the other person's ability to help himself and pursue his own path toward happiness.

Beware of helping people so much that they become overly dependent on you. It is more effective to engage in activities that help others help them discover and use their own strengths. (This is one reason why teaching a skill to others is often an especially gratifying volunteer experience.) Beware of confusing compassion with control and of trying to get others to do what you want in the name of "helping" them. When you try to control people, your ego becomes tied up in the outcome of events. That is the antithesis of no-strings-attached altruism and will most certainly not lead to happiness but to added stress and worry. Also, beware of enabling people to pursue self-destructive habits. You won't help a gambling addict by buying them a lottery ticket. You won't help a child you are tutoring by doing the homework they neglected to do.

Beware of volunteering for activities, or in settings that are poor matches for you. The situation may not be right for you if...

- You are not utilising any of your skills and strengths.

- You are experiencing a lot of anxiety (the usual beginner's adaptation aside).

- You are being assigned tasks that are over your head.

- You find the setting depersonalising.

- You are continually asked to do more, even if it means sapping time from your work or family.

- You are made to feel guilty when you cannot do more.

Beware of feeling bad if you cannot *"fix"* or *"solve"* everything. The idea that any one person can do so is irrational and will prevent you from achieving anything because you will be so completely overwhelmed by what you cannot do. Don't be too hard on yourself; remember, you didn't create the problem you are trying to alleviate. Keep things in perspective. Being altruistic does not mean you can save the world, or even *"save"* one person. You can support and assist people in their journey, but in the end everyone must take responsibility for their lives or they will not find their own pleasure and meaning. To begin helping, think small. In the words of William Blake, it is best to be helpful in *"minute particulars."*

Try to keep your ego out of the helping process. Examine your motivation. If you are performing altruistic acts so that others will notice and praise your sacrifice and *"selflessness,"* you are setting yourself up for disappointment and unhappiness. There is nothing wrong with recognition, but you will gain more contentment if you neither expect it nor think of it as your ultimate goal. Finally, remember that kindness begins when you are kind to yourself.

Beware of overdoing your altruism to the point of burning out. Compassion starts with self-compassion. In the Buddhist tradition, even meditation on compassion (known as the practice of metta, or *"loving kindness,"* begins with affirming one's compassion for oneself). The practitioner begins by silently repeating the phrase, *"May I be happy; may I be at peace."* Only then do they begin to direct the phrase toward loved ones and then ultimately to all: *"May all beings be happy; may all beings be at peace."* The progression of this meditation demonstrates the importance of carefully caring for ourselves. If we don't, we will be too stressed, tired, and overwhelmed to effectively care for anyone else.

When we help in healthy ways we do not feel pressured or burned out. We feel satisfied and gratified. And the more satisfied and gratified we feel, the more we will continue to help.

This is a highly positive feedback loop. If we give it a chance to initiate, we are likely to make helping a regular part of our life as opposed to an occasional dabbling. That consistency will, in turn, help to insulate us from the effects of stress and from a buildup of negative emotions. Certainly it won't take away stress or sadness (these things are a part of life), but engaging in altruism will, over time, make us more optimistic and resilient.

We often think of life as a zero-sum game, the kind of endeavour where someone must win (and be happy) and someone must lose (and be unhappy). But this does not appear to be the case. In fact, just the opposite appears to be true: the more we make others happy, the happier we are likely to be.

"It is one of the most beautiful compensations of this life that no man can sincerely try to help another without helping himself."—Ralph Waldo Emerson

Today, science has confirmed what spiritual teachers have long expounded. The Golden Rule of happiness works precisely because there is more than enough happiness to go around. And one true *"secret of happiness"* is that we are happy when we make others happy.

CHAPTER 3
ELEMENTS OF
HAPPINESS

TEN

Laughing

The ability to appreciate and generate humour is a character trait that has attracted special interest from those who study happiness—no doubt because humour has so many beneficial effects. There is nothing like a good, hearty laugh to make us feel both instant emotional cheer and immediate physical release.

But humour is also a way to bond with others and enhance our social connections. Perhaps most significant of all, humour can help us rise above our troubles, maintain perspective and flexibility, and even re-evaluate our circumstances in a new, more positive light.

The Physiology of Laughter

Part of the curative power of humour is purely physiological. It has to do with the impact of laughter on our bodies and our brains.

Laughter is a form of eustress—that is, of positive stress (that's *"eu"* as in euphoria). It's a stimulus that brings body and brain to an alert state. But unlike distress or negative stress, which generates anxiety, it's helpful rather than harmful. It makes us feel alive, vibrant, and "up."

Humour and Social Connection

Humour's benefits also extend into the social realm. Humour helps us build and maintain bonds with others—bonds that are themselves essential to happiness.

To see how this works, consider it from an evolutionary perspective. Why do we humans appreciate humour and why do we laugh in the first place? What on Earth did Mother Nature have in mind?

Social Survival

Some primates other than humans (such as chimpanzees and bonobos, our close genetic relations) exhibit grins and sounds that signal availability for friendly social interaction. But humans appear to be the only species that exhibits full-fledged laughter (aptly termed social playization by anthropologists) as a routine part of communication and not simply as a response to physical stimulation (such as tickling).

Communicative laughter probably evolved as our ancestors climbed down from the treetops in search of new habitats. At this important turning point, laughter served a number of critical social purposes:

- It signalled to other group members when an environment was safe and free of predators.

- It let everyone know it was an appropriate time to relax.

- It enhanced the trust and cooperation needed to take risks as a group.

- It eased individuals' sense of isolation or loneliness— especially because the sound of laughter carries across relatively long distances.

We may have left the treetop canopy behind long ago, but we still use laughter as a mechanism to fulfil all these very necessary functions. We use it to decrease social stress. We use it to reassure. We use it to motivate. We use it to bond.

Social Success

We are much more likely to laugh in social situations than alone. If you don't believe this, try watching your favourite Seinfeld rerun alone and then with friends. On which occasion did you laugh louder, longer, and more frequently? Most people would probably agree they laughed a good deal more with companions. That's because they're not only taking pleasure from the antics of the characters, but also communicating to others—saying, in effect, *"Hey, I can relate to that, can't you?"*

Laughter is wordless conversation. This powerful dialogue begins when we are babies, bonding with parents, who simply cannot resist eliciting our endearing giggles. It continues throughout childhood, facilitating friendships. And it pays a powerful role in the mating game, where humour can be a potent flirtation strategy. (Check out personal ads to see how many romance seekers cite *"a sense of humour"* as essential in a potential boyfriend or girlfriend.) Throughout life, in virtually any setting, humour and laughter can make pleasant situations more pleasant and unpleasant ones more tolerable. It can grease the wheels of negotiation in a tough business setting. It can help sway a jury. It can win voters over to a politician.

Humour can do all these things because we are far less likely to feel separate from people when we are laughing with them. There is nothing like a shared laugh to instantly communicate, *"You and I are on the same wavelength."* It is also, in the moment that we are laughing with someone, virtually impossible to feel hatred or fear toward them. Even when the moment passes, residual good feeling lingers. How bad can someone be, after all, if we both "get it"?

Not all kinds of humour lead to bonding. While self-deprecating humour says you are self-aware, humble, and empathic, humour that denigrates others marks you as cruel and insensitive. If bonding is your social goal, go for healthy laughs, avoid sarcasm, and avoid eliciting sneers and jeers. Remember, there's a difference between laughing with someone versus at them.

Laughter as Reward

Experiencing a social laugh is good. Even better, perhaps, is the happy feeling of reward we get from instigating one. When we make someone laugh, we have a feeling of instant success. And if the situation was a potentially thorny one, we feel a sense of relief as well.

When we intentionally and successfully make others laugh, we feel confident, brimming with self-esteem. Their laughter is, in effect, an invitation to go onto continue communicating. When we make a crowd laugh we can feel like *"king of the world,"* as though we have everyone in the palm of our hand. And indeed, for a moment, we actually do.

Choosing to See the Light Side

Sometimes laughter erupts spontaneously, but sometimes we can make a conscious choice to see the humour in a situation. When we do so, we are consciously reframing our experience and, in a very real sense, choosing a positive interpretation over a negative one.

We have all experienced times in our lives when we *"don't know whether to laugh or cry."* Exasperated and frustrated by circumstances, uncooperative people, maddening machinery—or all those things together—we throw up our hands. We might not actually cry, but we might grit our teeth, hunch our shoulders, and clench our fists in classic stress-saturated poses. But what if we actively reframed our experience so that we could stop stressing and laugh instead? This may seem unlikely, but chances are you have already done this—albeit with a bit of a time lag. Surely there were events in your life that seemed hopeless and when you felt helpless: pubescent crushes that weren't reciprocated, job interviews that went painfully awry, plans that didn't work out no matter how hard you tried. But as time passes, you have probably learned to see some of the humour in those situations—especially if, in the end, they all worked out for the best. (Who would have wanted to marry their first crush anyway?)

Moreover, you have probably transformed these events, once perceived as negative, into some of your funniest stories—those tales you tell about yourself that are always bound to incite warm laughter and nods of understanding.

Now the challenge is to try and appreciate some of life's frustrations and even its absurdities as they are unfolding. If we interpret them with a humorous bent, we can transcend the negative feelings that we might typically attach to them.

So, the next time you *"don't know whether to laugh or cry,"* or perhaps when you simply feel like screaming, try one of these strategies:

- Create a late-night monologue. If you're stranded at an airport while your luggage has moved on without you, or if you're trying to get off *"hold"* in an automated telephone system and speak to a human being, imagine retelling the story later that night to an appreciative audience. What would Jimmy Fallon or David Letterman say to get everyone to recognize their *"pain"* and laugh it away?

- Jot down your jokes. Office air-conditioning conked out on the hottest day of the year? How hot was it? Go on, take a stab at it. You can amuse yourself, and may even come up with something so good you'll want to share it.

- Find an immediate audience. Stuck in an interminable line at the Department of Motor Vehicles? Find someone ahead of you or behind you who looks like they need cheering up, and then say something to make them smile.

- Grin while you bear it. Even if you're all alone in your plight, try to find something humorous about it and smile. The mere act of smiling will brighten your mood and make you feel happier.

Finding the humour in a situation that could *"go either way"* is empowering. It gives you a greater sense of control over whatever situation you are in. That sense of control can, in turn, help you maintain an upbeat frame of mind.

Do You Get It?

As with most traits and behaviours, the ability to appreciate humour, and to generate humour, comes to each of us in varying degrees. Underlying genetic factors may influence how often and how enthusiastically we tend to laugh. Animal researchers can actually determine which individuals in a population of lab rats are most playful and most receptive to tickling, and then breed for these traits. In humans, it's been noted that babies born with extroverted temperaments tend to do more laughing than those with introverted temperaments.

In the Western world, the country where people laugh the most is Italy. Supposedly the average Italian devotes 21 minutes a day to laughter.

Of course, it has never occurred to most of us to count our outbursts of laughter. But what if you tried? Try keeping a laugh diary, or devising a simple system such as making a checkmark in your day planner or putting a coin in a jar each time you laugh out loud? This would give you a rough idea of your *"humour benchmark."*

While you're at it, give yourself a point for each time you make someone else laugh, be they family member, friend, co-worker, or total stranger. That not only makes you happy, but gives to others.

Enhancing Humour Appreciation

No matter how much you laugh in adulthood, chances are you laughed more as a child. Those same experts who peg the average number of daily adult laughs at 15 for grown-ups say that many small children laugh hundreds of times a day. Based on this, each of us has the potential to laugh—and to generate and share laughter—more. Here are some ways to do so:

- Create a video humour library. Collect DVDs of movies and television shows that you find hilarious, no matter how many times you watch them. Fill some shelves with these comic gems, and remind yourself to insert one when you need a lift in spirits.

- Leave funny books and magazines around the house. Leave these in strategic spots that will make them easy to access—on coffee tables, the bedside stand, or in the bathroom.

- Share a *"funniest ever"* list. Now that you have identified the materials that make you laugh most, make a list and share it with friends. Ask them to do the same. You all might discover a few new films and books that crack you up.

- Write a humour bio. Give yourself an assignment to write down the funniest (in retrospect!) things that have ever happened to you. You'll make yourself laugh while reminding yourself that things often work out for the best. Now you'll also have plenty of material to amuse your friends with.

- Keep a *"You Said It"* jar. Keep your ear out for *"funny and true"* aphorisms that strike a chord with you. (For example, Steve Jobs offered a piece of advice in a commencement speech that advised everyone to *"live every day as it was your last—because someday you'll be right."*) Write them on slips of paper and store them in a jar for when you need some quick, philosophical, and funny advice.

- Hang out with the light-hearted. Seek out companions who like fun, who are funny, and who are ready, willing, and able to laugh. Limit your exposure to grouches, whiners, and fussers.

- Socialize in big groups. Research shows that the larger the group, the more likely laughter is to occur. Just as you're more likely to catch a cold in a big group, you're more likely to *"catch"* a laugh. (Don't worry about the cold part. Remember that laughter boosts your immunity.)

If you're not in the mood to laugh, you can seek a structured class that will help you "fake it 'til you make it." During the past decade, workshops in a practice known as laughter yoga have been catching on in settings as diverse as corporations, hospitals, schools, and even military installations. The practice is said to benefit emotional and physical well-being, which combines yogic breathing exercises and heavy doses of group mirth. Though practitioners at first generate laughter "without a reason," the contrived laughter invariably leads to genuine laughter.

Increasing your capacity for humour and laughter will help you feel more relaxed and more optimistic. It will help you develop empathy and be more sensitive to others—and thus improve your relationships. All in all, humour is a potent tonic for maintaining a happiness-enhancing perspective.

ELEVEN

Optimism

"A year from now you may wish you had started today."

Karen Lamb

Is happiness a self-fulfilling prophecy? To a large degree, the answer seems to be yes. Research shows that people who are optimists—that is, those who are inclined to expect good outcomes—are more content, more resilient, and have fewer physical and emotional disorders than pessimists who anticipate negative outcomes.

But there's good news for pessimists (at least for those willing to hear it). A bleak outlook can be transformed. Research also shows that it is possible to become more optimistic.

The Happy Rewards of Optimism

For a long time optimists were not much studied by psychology. As with most people who were doing pretty well, they were not considered squeaky wheels that needed grease. For many decades we knew a lot more about pessimists and how their penchant for feeling helpless created anxiety, depression, and—in the end—increased helplessness itself. Today, however, psychologists acknowledge there is a lot to learn from optimists. To illustrate what some of those things are, consider the following scenario.

A Matter of Attitude

Jill, a pessimist, and Jane, an optimist, each go to their physician for an annual check-up and take a number of routine tests. They are both called the following day and told that the results of one of the tests was irregular and they need to retake it the following week it to see if there is a problem. *"Don't worry,"* they are told. *"We sometimes get false positives, and that is why we want you to retake the test."*

Jill interprets the situation as negative from the moment she gets the call. She assumes that the test will show she has a dire medical condition, which she begins researching on the Internet immediately. Preoccupied with what she is sure is a grave illness, she begins sleeping poorly and losing focus at work. She snaps at her co-workers and at her spouse. (If only they knew my terrible fate, she thinks!) All week long her mood plummets and she becomes more and more nervous.

Jane also feels an initial pang of anxiety as she puts down the phone. But she counsels herself to take to heart the advice not to worry, that such tests can give a false result.

She goes on about her business, and if a stressful thought intrudes she reminds herself that everything will turn out fine. Even if the test turns out to reveal a problem, she is confident that she will be successfully treated and that those around her will help her with their love and support. Things tend to work out, she remembers, but if there's an issue, I can deal with whatever comes my way.

If the results of the second test indicate that Jill and Jane are both perfectly fine, Jane, the optimist, would think, I knew that was nothing to be concerned about. But Jill, the pessimist, would have already suffered a significant amount of stress, grown fatigued and irritable, alienated those close to her, and generally became miserable. By force of habit, she would simply start to worry about something else, such as, What if the second test was wrong? But what if the tests indicated there was an illness after all? You might think that Jill would fare better, because she had prepared herself for the worst. But in fact, her spirits would likely sink further as she affirmed her belief that nothing ever goes right. Jane, on the other hand, would, after experiencing some initial let-down, mobilize her considerable internal resources and her external support system and determine that she would vanquish her illness. Even if she had setbacks, she would count her blessings. All other things being equal between her treatment and Jill's, her positive attitude could be a significant factor in her recovery.

The Optimist's Advantage

Things can go well or badly for optimists or pessimists alike—the difference is in the reaction. Optimists tend to fare better and feel happier in any circumstance:

- They avoid anticipating the worst, limiting their stress and the toxic biochemical reactions that stress can trigger.

- They exhibit a variety of active coping strategies.

- They have more positive relationships (and thus more social support) because they are more trusting and cooperative.

- Although they may certainly experience emotional distress, they are not immobilized by it, do not let it impair their judgment, and tend to rebound quickly.

- They not only bounce back from crises faster than pessimists, but bounce back to a more positive and energetic level than where they started out.

Optimists even outlive pessimists: studies show that they have higher immunity and that optimism appears to reduce the risk and lessen the severity of cardiovascular disease, pulmonary disease, hypertension, diabetes, and colds and upper respiratory infections.

There is even a strong case to be made that optimists play a part in creating some of the positive outcomes they anticipate. To prove that positive expectations can help shape reality, consider the placebo effect. In every study of a potentially helping drug, a certain number of subjects are given an inert sugar pill—a placebo—instead of actual medication. Typically, about a third of these subjects improve even though their cure was a *"fake."* Likewise, many subjects who are told they are being given pain relief medication—when in fact they are being given a placebo— immediately report a decrease in pain. Their brains have actually kicked in and produced more endorphins, which are natural pain relievers.

Putting a Happy Spin on the World

So what exactly makes one an optimist? Once again, heredity can get the ball rolling. A study that measured the optimism of identical and fraternal twins showed a higher correlation of attitudes between identical twins, which suggests that genetics may play a substantial role in predisposing us toward embracing a glass-half-full outlook. But even those who conducted the study acknowledge that optimism is a complex trait that can be transmitted by indirect means. We can learn to be more optimistic, for example, from optimistic role models— especially those who are close to us, such as our parents.

Explanatory style is the way we explain the causes and effects of our circumstances to ourselves. It is the "spin" we put on events that occur in our lives.

But what behaviours would these role models be modelling? What would we emulate to become more optimistic? Martin Seligman, Christopher Peterson (Peterson, Maier, & Seligman, Learned Helplessness, 1996), and other leading psychologists contend that we can start moving toward a more optimistic outlook by noticing and addressing our explanatory style.

Now versus Always

One of the key factors that make an optimist an optimist, according to Seligman (Seligman, 1991), is their ability to view negative events as temporary. Pessimists, on the other hand, view them as permanent.

Feeling tired?

If you're a pessimist you'd say, *"I'll never have the same energy I used to."* If you're an optimist you'd be more likely to say, *"I feel tired today; I'm sure it will pass with a good night's sleep."*

Sick of a long, rainy spell?

If you're a pessimist you'd say, *"Climate change has ruined the weather patterns around here for good."* If you're an optimist you'd probably say, *"I'll really appreciate the sunshine when it comes."*

Disappointed with yourself because you cheated on your weight-loss diet?

If you're a pessimist you'd say, *"I knew it. I might as well throw those skinny jeans away."* If you're an optimist you'd slap yourself on the wrist and say, *"I'm getting right back on the wagon—and not the chow wagon!"*

When negative events occur, pessimists insist that they're always wrong, that they'll never succeed, that they're constantly failing, that their slump will last forever, and that they are unlucky all the time. Optimists, on the other hand, will tell you they made a mistake this time, that they're in a slump at the moment, or that things didn't work out so well today—but their luck is bound to change.

However, it's important to note that optimists have a wonderful way of altering their perspective so that it stays cheerful. That means that when things go right, they are more than willing to switch scripts. On a roll, an optimist will foresee that fortuitous circumstances will endure. They'll remark that their luck is holding, as usual, and that they were right again.

Although this is a flip-flop, it is an effective perspective. Optimists limit the distress caused by negative events by minimizing the perception of their duration, and they maximize pleasant and positive events by refusing to dwell on their impermanence.

Situational versus Universal

Optimists also differ from pessimists in that they view negative events as being limited in scope. When one thing goes wrong, they see it as an anomaly. They don't leap to the conclusion that this occurrence is indicative of everything going wrong. They compartmentalize their troubles, putting borders around them rather than letting them bleed into other areas.

Someone tells you they don't like your new haircut?

If you're an optimist you'll shrug it off: *"Bob doesn't like my new haircut (that jerk!)."* If you're a pessimist you're apt to conclude, *"Nobody likes my haircut; I look awful."*

Romantic interest cooling things off?

If you're an optimist you'll think, *"I'll find someone better."* If you're a pessimist you'll practically convince yourself to join a monastery.

But when things go right, get ready for a style switch again. An optimist in a good relationship says, *"I deserve great relationships. I'm a desirable person."* The pessimist says,

"This person seems to like me—I wonder what's wrong with them?"

The tendency to assess isolated negative events as indicators of ongoing and pervasive problems predisposes pessimists to give up before they give themselves a chance to succeed. Numerous studies confirm that optimists are more likely to stick with tasks, stay with their jobs, and perform better at their work than pessimists do.

Internal Causes versus External Causes

The third side of the optimism versus pessimism explanatory style triangle has to do with exhibiting a kind of self-serving bias. Optimists take credit for their successes, but attribute failure to external factors. Pessimists conclude that successes are due to external factors and that failures are "all their fault."

Got a good grade on an exam?

If you're an optimist you'll attribute it to your innate intelligence: *"Of course I got an A; I work hard."* If you're a pessimist you'll attribute your grade to the fact that "the test was not hard" or that *"the teacher is an easy grader."*

Scored a goal in the big game?

If you're an optimist you'll cite your strength and skill. If you're a pessimist you'll cite your opponent's momentary lapse in judgment or attention.

Now for the flip side: optimists who fail a test or miss a goal wouldn't be likely to attribute this to a personal internal flaw. They might say the test was unfair or the referee made a bad call (both external causes). They might say they had a bad day (thus relegating the event to one-time status). They might even say they need to study more or practice harder (thus putting the matter within their sphere of personal control). What they do not do is associate poor outcomes with internal shortcomings. Optimists might sometimes lose, but they never see themselves as *"losers."*

Now, if you're starting to wonder whether an optimistic perspective can go too far or may be blind to reality, ultimately creating problems and unhappiness, you're asking a valid question which we'll address later in this chapter.

In Search of Optimism

Is there a way to tell if you're more of an optimist than a pessimist? And can you become more optimistic? The answer to both questions is yes. Psychologists who wish to determine someone's explanatory style can do so by administering an Attributional Style Questionnaire (ASQ), which measures one's level of optimistic versus pessimistic responses and identifies prevalent attitudes. But happiness researchers also became interested in the styles of people who weren't going to take any such test. They wondered: Which sports heroes are optimists? Which politicians? Which business leaders? And how does that optimism affect their performance?

This curiosity led to Dr. Christopher Peterson's pioneering work in what has become known as the CAVE technique: Content Analysis of Verbatim Explanations. The idea is actually very simple—so simple that Peterson began Caving by reading the sports pages. If a player or coach lost a game, Petersen noted whether or not they blamed external factors (for example, inclement weather) or put the onus on themselves. He noted whether they viewed the defeat as part of a trend or as an exception. He used the participants' direct quotations to create explanatory style profiles. Later researchers began caving a broad range of material, spoken and written—speeches, interviews, press conferences, diaries, letters, and even wills. Using the technique they could determine the pessimistic or optimistic tendencies of virtually anyone, living or deceased. An excellent beginning strategy for anyone who would like to move toward the more optimistic end spectrum should begin observing their own communications by using a similar technique.

Developing Self-Awareness

What kinds of things do you typically say when things go wrong? Some of us are not even aware when we default to a pessimistic stance. Yet out of habit we might say things such as, *"I just can't win," "I can never get a break,"* or *"That's just my luck"* when things go wrong. We might greet a setback by responding, *"Isn't that always the way it is?"* We might greet bad news by waiting for the other shoe to drop, by asking *"What next?"* or by citing Murphy's Law: *"Whatever can go wrong will go wrong."* (Murphy was no optimist!) On the other hand we might have our optimistic moments—ones we can notice and expand on. As with those times when we react to negative events by noting that this too shall pass, or, as Scarlet O'Hara put it, *"Tomorrow's another day."* (Scarlet never gave in to pessimism. Where some take lemons and make lemonade, she took a pair of drapes and made a velvet ball gown.) Now, what do you typically say when things go right? Do you react with an optimistic *"Now we're cooking!"* or a pessimistic *"This will never last,"* or *"Well, at least one thing went right"*? Do you say, *"I made it happen,"* or do you chalk it up to dumb luck?

Self-awareness is the first step on the road to change. Chart your responses to events during a brief period of time, even as little as a week or two, and it can yield some remarkable insights.

The Attitude-Outcome Link

Becoming aware of your habitual reactions to events is a first step on the road to change. The second is to acknowledge the link between your attitudes, your actions, and your outcomes.

Here's how it works: attitudes fuel our beliefs. Beliefs fuel our expectations. And when we expect something to happen, we—deliberately or unwittingly—take actions that contribute to making it happen.

Let's say your boss ignores a memo you sent requesting that you be assigned to an exciting new project team. As a pessimist, you might assume you will never be assigned to a dynamic team, that your career is going nowhere, that you are clearly not made of the "right stuff" your boss is looking for, and that you might even get fired. You never raise the subject of this team again, and in fact never bother to volunteer for anything. You decide to "stay under the radar." Obviously this strategy is not going to help you win your boss's favour. In the end, you could lose your job—just like you thought.

On the other hand, an optimist might have assumed her boss simply didn't recognize how valuable she is and what she has to contribute. She would try again to be assigned to the team—perhaps approaching the boss in person rather than by e-mail. And if she didn't get what she wanted this time, she would assume this was an anomaly. Convinced she would get assigned to the next big project, she would make sure she did good work that got noticed. Optimists look for solutions to problems!

If you notice that your attitudes are leading to actions that are detrimental to you, try acting as if you had a more optimistic attitude. Ask yourself, what would an optimist do here? Then try it. What you will in fact be doing is limiting your susceptibility to a sense of helplessness and giving yourself more power to control your circumstances.

Handling Negative Thoughts

Making a shift toward increased pessimism is a process, not an overnight *"miracle cure."* Negative thoughts won't simply vanish, and it's important to note that even optimists have them. But it's what they do with them that matters. Should habitual negative thoughts persist, try one or more of these techniques:

Argue with yourself. Acknowledge your feelings. Then, allow yourself to logically dispute them. It's not rational to think that one lost game will ruin the season. Getting a "C" in this course does not mean I am stupid—I need more time to prepare. Substitute affirmations for rumination. If you find yourself getting stuck on a negative thought, convert it to its opposite and create an affirmation instead. Let's say you are sitting on an airplane next to someone with a head cold. You notice yourself thinking, *"Now I'm going to get a cold, too"*. But now that you've noticed, try telling yourself, I have health and well-being. It's most effective to phrase your affirmation in the positive. Saying *"I will not get a cold"* is phrased in the negative and can still conjure up anxiety.

Stop before you act on negative feelings. Always remember that having a feeling is completely different from acting on that feeling. Negative consequences arise from actions. Take positive actions no matter how you feel, and pat yourself on the back for the positive consequences you generate.

Try combining optimism and altruism. When you catch yourself saying something pessimistic, "fine" yourself a quarter and put it in a jar. At the end of each month, roll up your quarters and donate the proceeds to a charitable cause. Now you have actively converted something negative into something positive. You'll not only gain awareness of your habitual explanations, but also get a "helper's high." Some people have made this a family project, encouraging everyone in their household to participate.

Retrospective Optimism

A recent research trend points to yet another potential strategy for increasing one's level of optimism. This research centres on personal narrative, the stories that each of us tell about our own lives and how we got to where we are today. To conduct this research, psychologists at Northwestern University conducted two-hour, life-story interviews. Typically, subjects describe phases of their lives as if they were outlining chapters from childhood through adolescence to middle age. They also describe a number of pivotal scenes in detail, including high points (winning that scholarship); low points (being left at the altar); and turning points (deciding to go to law school rather than medical school). When the transcripts were analysed, researchers noted some interesting trends. Those with mood-related problems reported negative details even in predominantly positive memories (I spoke at my graduation, although the day would have been better without the rain) and tend to close *"chapters"* on notes of disappointment. On the other hand, those whom researchers called generative adults (energetic, involved, and civic-minded) tended to focus on themes of redemption (I got left at the altar but on a trip to recover met the man of my dreams). These life stories shape not only how we think about ourselves, but also how we behave, those behind the studies say. But these narratives are not set in stone. As it turns out, each of us is gradually but continually revising our story treatments—and therein lies their potential to benefit us.

Those who have studied the power of these personal narratives contend that interpretations of past behaviour shape how we envision the future. If we go back and revise our tales with a more positive bent—noting how challenges led to growth and failures led to new opportunity—we are likely to look forward with a more positive attitude.

Many successful people display retrospective optimism when they recount their life stories. Steve Jobs, for example, gave a widely quoted commencement address at Stanford in which he described three potentially devastating events-dropping out of college, being fired from his own company, and receiving a cancer diagnosis—as integral to his growth and vision. Reading autobiographies and speeches by those who recount their stories in this sort of light can help us tap the influence of positive role models.

Tapping the power of positive memory is not dissimilar to changing one's explanatory style in the present. Indeed, accomplishing the first task can help us accomplish the second. As we recall times when we emerged victorious from life's challenges, we can build a reservoir of confidence with which to ground ourselves as new challenges present themselves—and we can use those challenges as chances to achieve resilience and, ultimately, happiness.

Optimistic Realism

Having a firm grasp on reality has long been considered the gold standard of mental health, but we can acknowledge that optimists are biased in a self-serving way. They are not completely objective when it comes to evaluating risks, which in extreme cases could lead to, say, an optimistic cigarette smoker continuing to smoke despite evidence that doing so is detrimental to her health, or an investor sinking his life savings into a new and unproven investment scheme.

This is a conundrum that has led to many further studies of optimistic perspectives and their limitations. Researchers now suggest that there may be an optimal margin of illusion that, while allowing people to slightly overestimate their abilities and chances of success, does not typically lead to irresponsible behaviours based on false assumptions.

In other words, balance is the key. Optimism and realism need not be mutually exclusive terms. Optimists may be more inclined to take a calculated risk, but those who plunge headlong into situations of immeasurable uncertainty based on an inflated understanding of their skills or their luck are not optimists. They could more accurately be described as narcissists with grandiose delusions. Most situations in life allow room for some ambiguity. Given the same set of facts, we can still legitimately speculate about outcomes. For example, a group of scientists who agree that climate change is occurring may be divided into one group that sees the problem as insoluble and one that sees it as reversible. Both groups can offer objective evidence that backs up what they see as their logical assessment. Yet the group that sees the problem as reversible is, of course, the group likely to seek solutions. In this situation, as in so many others, *"truth"* is an imprecise commodity, yet this latter group is willing to act on its interpretation of the truth in an optimistic, proactive way. (Note that their attitude is we can do it, rather than it will happen. They are not betting on a magical outcome, but planning to address genuine obstacles and challenges.) Optimistic thinking will not lead to long-term happiness if it isn't based in reality. But being a realistic optimist is possible. Realistic optimism requires not ignoring facts, but collecting and evaluating available information as thoroughly as possible before acting constructively to potentially maximize positive outcomes.

When there is still some level of uncertainty (as is the case in most situations), realistic optimists...

- Give the benefit of the doubt when considering others' motivations.

- Remain alert to positive elements in the current situation—even while acknowledging the existence of negative elements.

- Accept the challenges that lie ahead while holding on to hope.

Finally, it's important to note that maintaining realistic optimism requires regular reality checks. The successful optimist will not just set a plan in motion and hope for the best. They will set interim goals, solicit feedback from knowledgeable sources, and alter their strategy when doing so is called for. Nevertheless, the attitudes that realistic optimists hold about past, present, and future eschew cynicism, complaint, and stagnation in favour of trust, gratitude, and goal-setting. The latter are the habits of the happy.

TWELVE

Gratitude

"This is a wonderful day. I've never seen this one before."

Maya Angelou

A number of research groups have studied the effects of asking people to stop and ponder, as a matter of routine, what they are grateful for in their lives. The experiments often involve instructing people to take a few minutes at the end of each day to enumerate what happened during the day that was good, and to write or recite a phrase expressing gratitude for those things. The things that inspire gratitude can be major events (I'm grateful I found out I'm getting a promotion; I'm thankful that my kid got into a great college), but more often than not they are relatively minor (I'm thankful that I got to take my dog for a long, enjoyable walk; I'm so glad we got the kitchen faucet fixed). Even if someone's day was disappointing or frustrating or even downright unpleasant, the assignment holds: give thanks for the good. (Today it rained buckets—I'm thankful because my lawn needs watering.)

The results of these experiments show that people who make such a practice a part of their lives report increased happiness and diminished symptoms of depression. The follow-up findings of one such experiment, the *"three good things"* study, which asked participants to list each evening three things that went well and why, were especially interesting. Sixty percent of the subjects in the experiment said they were still ending each day this way six months after the experiment ended. To them, the ongoing benefits were obvious.

Don't assume that only those you might consider "lucky" are adept at expressing gratitude. Individuals who have been through the most trying experiences and weathered the most adverse circumstances are often the most grateful. Hurricane and other natural disaster survivors, for example, tend to express gratitude for what they have not lost.

A Gallup survey of American adults and teenagers found that 95 percent of respondents felt at least somewhat happy when expressing gratitude and more than 50 percent felt extremely happy while doing so. But science shows that the joy that comes from being grateful lasts longer than it takes to utter or to jot down one's sentiments. An attitude of gratitude is cumulative—it tends to accrue long-term benefits. Those who display such an attitude have been shown to be energetic, optimistic, and empathetic, and even to enjoy significant physical well-being.

Anchoring in the Present

Where does the power of gratitude lie? The very act of giving thanks requires us to stop, look around, and notice where we are and what we have right now. It brings us into the present moment and makes us more conscious of what surrounds us. It frees us from ruminating about past problems or focusing on future-oriented anxieties. During much of our existence, we may take things for granted, but in these moments of taking stock we allow ourselves to be pleasantly surprised: Look at all of this! When we choose to focus on positive aspects of our immediate situation, we acknowledge small but significant good things that might otherwise have passed unnoticed.

It's been said that if happy people painted pictures of their lives, positive elements would be in the foreground, while negative ones would constitute a vague and fuzzy backdrop. Gratitude helps us achieve just this sort of perspective. If we make it a habit to find things to be grateful for, almost anything can be considered a blessing compared to the worst-case scenario. You may dislike your boss, for example, but that can be reframed as I am grateful to have a job. You may have broken your arm in an accident, but that translates to, I'm glad I walked away alive!

"Let us rise up and be thankful, for if we didn't learn a lot today, at least we learned a little, and if we didn't learn a little, at least we didn't get sick, and if we got sick, at least we didn't die; so, let us all be thankful." -Buddha

Gaining Security

We can always chase more riches and comforts in the name of attaining security. But this continually grasping state of mind has been shown to detract from happiness. Genuine security entails feeling satisfied with where we are. And although being happy certainly doesn't preclude setting goals, it does mean not being a slave to social pressure or being obsessed by financial status.

Reminding ourselves what we have to be grateful for in the moment can help quell the urge to jump on that hedonic treadmill. It can also remind us to honour ourselves for having gotten as far as we have—and that reminder, in turn, makes us more secure in our own strengths and abilities.

Enhancing Altruism

In keeping with the *"feel good, do good"* effect, people who feel grateful tend to be highly helpful and nurturing to others. It is as if by counting our own blessings we remember the value of being a blessing to someone else. In addition, gratitude can help sustain those whose acts of caregiving might lead to physical and emotional strain. A study of caregivers who were under the stress of caring for severely ill loved ones showed that those who took the time to write about their gratitude remained in a better state of health themselves.

Lowering Stress, Upping Immunity

Feelings of thankfulness and appreciation have been shown to contribute to overall well-being in a number of ways. Studies show...

- They stimulate our parasympathetic nervous system— the part of our autonomic nervous system that initiates relaxation—and *"puts on the brakes"* in the aftermath of frustration or anxiety—by lowering heart rate, respiration rate, and blood pressure.

- They increase levels of an immune antibody called IgA (immunoglobulin A), which is part of the body's first line of defence against invading microbes— especially those that cause upper respiratory infections.

- They stimulate the release of a beneficial hormone called DHEA (dehydroepiandosterone), a hormone said to play a role in weight maintenance and in prolonging youthful energy.

- They correspond to a decrease in the stress-related hormone Cortisol, which can raise blood sugar to dangerous levels and cause other adverse health effects when released during sustained periods.

Feelings of gratitude not only help prevent illness, but play a role in helping us heal from illness and recover from surgery. In other words, those who feel thankful in spite of infirmities are most likely to rebound from them sooner.

Expressing Gratitude

When you were a child, your parents probably taught you that it was good and proper to say *"thank you."* Most of us still honour this social protocol. If someone holds a door open or helps us carry an unwieldy package or pays us a compliment, we say *"thanks"* in passing. There's nothing wrong with that, of course. However, you're likely to up your happiness quotient significantly if you also make it a point to express gratitude in deliberate, regular—perhaps even daily—ways.

Gratitude Journals

One way to ritualize the expression of thankfulness in your life is to keep what's become known as a gratitude journal. Doing so is a popular assignment in psychology courses, but many people are doing it at the behest of their church or synagogue, or simply trying the practice because they've read about it or heard about it through word of mouth.

The process is simple. Devote a notebook to the daily recordings of things for which you are thankful. Set aside some time at the end of each day to record a list of blessings in your life. These can be ongoing blessings, events from the past that have led to good things in the present or specific events that occurred in the course of the day. In short, they can be about anything that makes you feel grateful.

You can direct your items toward an individual (I am grateful to my sister Sarah for driving our Mom to the doctor) or to a spiritual figure (making your list a prayerful experience) or to no one in particular (a blanket acknowledgement to the universe at large).

No subject is off-limits in a gratitude journal. No topic is too small or inconsequential. You may be grateful that you have a hot cup of tea while you write, grateful that your beloved cat is curled on your lap, even grateful for the air you breathe or for the opportunity to enjoy some sweet dreams when you finish your writing.

From time to time you should read over your gratitude journal. Chances are you will be heartened by how many positive things you have in your life that you have begun to notice, appreciate, and savour. You may also wish to share some of the writings in your gratitude journal with your spouse or significant other. Couples who do so confirm this can have a profoundly positive effect on their relationship to bring them closer together.

Writing in a gratitude journal or offering up prayers or similar expressions of gratitude is best done at night. When the day is done we can review it with the aim of discovering the good that it contained. We will be more apt to go to sleep in a positive frame of mind and to wake up in a positive frame of mind.

Grudges or Gratitude

Writing expressions of gratitude to a specific person can also have the beneficial effect of helping you to forgive any past imperfect behaviour on their part. Sure, your older sibling might have teased and tormented you sometimes, but by focusing on the times when they encouraged you, cheered you up, made you laugh, or set a high standard for you to emulate, you will minimize the negative by accentuating the positive.

Now, think about some of the people to whom you might owe a debt of gratitude who perhaps only indirectly or inadvertently helped you. For example:

- The boss who told you that you weren't right for a certain promotion and turned out to be correct in saying you were better suited to another profession—one you are now successful in.

- The athletic coach who was rough on you, insisting you could be in much better shape (which you now are).

- The college roommate who was incredibly competitive with you and got you so reciprocally competitive that you graduated with honours.

Think how surprised they would be to get a letter of thanks from you!

What will you gain by looking back over your life and considering how certain people whose actions seemed unfair, irritating, or even unreasonable at the time turned out to be just what the doctor ordered? Only a whole new perspective! You are likely to be more tolerant, patient, and forgiving—all traits that serve your personal happiness far more than the negative thoughts that occur when we carry grudges.

In fact, we don't call it carrying a grudge for nothing. Those destructive emotions can weigh us down.

Graciously Accepting Gratitude

Finally, what if you are the recipient of someone else's gratitude? It will probably make you very happy, but somehow we have gotten the idea that the polite thing to do when thanked is to minimize what you did. One of the ways we typically respond when someone thanks us is to say, *"Hey, it's nothing!"* (The Spanish say *"de nada"* and the French say *"de Hen,"* which literally translate as *"it's nothing"* as well.)

But there are many other ways we can respond when someone says,

"Thank you very much":

"It means a lot to me to hear you say that."

"It was my pleasure."

"I appreciate your acknowledgement."

"You made my day!"

And of course,

"You are very welcome."

You may value humility, which is all well and good, but it is false humility to deny that you helped someone if you did.

Moreover it serves to diminish the effort that person took to express their gratitude in the first place. It is human nature to enjoy being appreciated. Whether you are on the giving or receiving end of gratitude, enjoy the happiness it brings.

THIRTEEN

Playfulness

"I will go anywhere as long as it is forward."

David Livingston

Imagine you are watching children at play. If someone asked you to describe their predominant feeling, chances are you would describe them as happy. And so they are. It's fun to play; to be truly playful is to be light-hearted and entranced.

Adults, too, have fun when they play. Play relaxes us and lifts our spirits. It relieves stress and takes our mind off our troubles. But, as this chapter shows, play can do even more to engender happiness. Play can help us lead not just a pleasant life, but also a life rich in engagement and meaning.

The Pleasure of Leisure

One of the most significant predictors of an individual's life satisfaction, research shows, is how much time that person spends engaged in leisure activities. The correlation is strong for many reasons.

The first and most obvious reason that leisure makes us happy is that many leisure activities directly produce pleasant sensations. If you like to run, bike, or swim, for example, you'll get all the mood-enhancing benefits that aerobic exercise provides—not to mention a boost to your health, vitality, and self-image. If you like to garden or fish or hike in the wilderness, you'll derive the aesthetic pleasures of being outdoors in restorative natural surroundings. If you like to listen to music, you'll also achieve mood enhancement: listening to quiet music raises feelings of contentment; listening to more stimulating music increases pleasurable arousal and excitement levels.

Recreational activities are also often done in the company of friends and family. Sometimes new friendships are formed or old ones strengthened by sharing leisure activities, from deep-sea diving to playing bridge. Because time spent with loved ones and friends is itself a potential source of happiness, leisure time can be doubly rewarding.

What we do with our leisure time can also help us build a sense of personal and community identity—both of which contribute to elevated feelings of self-worth and satisfaction. We enjoy describing ourselves in terms of what sport we prefer, identifying ourselves as golfers or sailors or surfers, and we often respond positively to those who pursue the same pastimes. There is an instant feeling of fraternity and a great deal to talk about. (Hey, you run marathons? I run marathons!) Sometimes we join formal organizations or clubs associated with our favourite activities, but even if we simply stand around and shoot the breeze in the most informal way, we appreciate and value the camaraderie.

Our leisure activities sometimes provide us with a chance to compete. If you thrive on competition, a rousing tennis match, an intense game of chess, or a video game tournament can afford you a special dose of hyper-alertness that's known as eustress—positive stress of brief, limited duration that our brains respond to with pleasure.

Of course, there is a seemingly endless variety of experiences that people enjoy in their nonworking hours. Some are interactive, others are solitary. Some take energy, some—such as watching television—are passive. What they all have in common is that they are activities we choose. No one insists we do them. And when our choice of how we spend our time is left to our own discretion that alone is enough to make us happy—at least to some degree.

But pleasurable leisure and recreation do not tell the whole story of the potential of play. Fun is fun—no one will argue with that. But play is a process that has even more to offer. Play can allow us to both lose ourselves—in the best sense— and, ultimately, to find ourselves.

The Higher Purposes of Play

Throughout much of the animal kingdom, play is a widespread phenomenon. If you've ever raised cats or dogs, their propensity for play is no doubt obvious to you. Dolphins also play, and so do chimps, bonobos, and other primates. When no immediate danger threatens and food is plentiful, many creatures spend the better part of their day at play.

Ethologists, researchers who study animal behaviour, including the behaviour of the human animal—note that play is anything but random. Indeed, it serves many evolutionary and developmental purposes. Play can be useful in developing survival skills, such as the ability to outfox or outrun a predator. It sharpens the mind by promoting mental strategizing. Play builds our ability to anticipate, weigh possible outcomes, and generate multiple solutions to problems. And play builds imagination, allowing the mind to wander and fantasize. Not all of our enjoyable leisure activities allow us to reach a highly engaged level that sharpens our saw, so to speak. And it's fine that not all of them do. There's nothing wrong with the simple, pleasant relaxation we derive from whiling away a Sunday afternoon browsing through catalogues or watching football. However, those who also integrate more demanding and creative endeavours into their repertoire of pastimes will reap additional benefits. When we engage in play that taps our drive and resourcefulness, we are apt to find ourselves entering the happy state known as *"flow."*

Couch potatoes take note: if you are spending all your leisure time in passive relaxation, you probably won't be as happy as you could be. When people are interrupted at random intervals to report how much they are enjoying themselves, those who are vegetating report far less satisfaction than those who are participating in an activity requiring physical or mental energy.

Going with the Flow

"Flow" is a concept formulated by Mihaly Csikszentmihalyi (Csikszentmihalyi M. , 1998), a University of Chicago professor. He defines flow, essentially, as an "optimal experience" that results from a maximally engaged state. Csikszentmihalyi observed this state in people engaged in activities as diverse as painting, sculpting, writing, dancing, playing or composing music, playing chess, and climbing mountains.

Flow is said to generate joy in those who achieve it. But this level of happiness far surpasses that experienced during transient diversions. It is deeper and extends far beyond the period that is actually devoted to the activity that brought it on in the first place. After being completely consumed by a flow-inducing experience, one emerges with a heightened sense of well-being and self-confidence.

Finding and pursuing an activity that brings on a state of flow is a means of expanding our potential for happiness. So, just how do you know when you're in flow?

Relishing a Challenge

Overwhelmingly, (Csikszentmihalyi & Nakamura, 2011) (Csikszentmihalyi M. , 1998) says, optimal experiences are reported during activities that require the investment of energy (mental, physical, or both) and present challenges that could not be met without the appropriate skills.

If one has the skills to pursue an activity, that activity or even the prospect of that activity becomes exciting. When involved in the pursuit, an adequately skilled person becomes engrossed in choosing from among myriad opportunities for action. For example, a rock climber must decide where to place his crampons so as not to take a tumble, and a writer must decide how to structure sentences and paragraphs so as to best convey mood and meaning.

If you're looking for flow, match the level of your skill to your chosen pursuit. If you are very good at something, make sure the specific activity is not too easy for you. And if you're competing, seek out worthy opponents. If what you're doing is a piece of cake, you won't be happy, you'll be bored.

If one does not have the skills to undertake a particular activity, then that activity lacks meaning. It becomes not challenging, but frustrating. For example, imagine attempting to complete a crossword puzzle in a foreign language. It would be pointless at best, infuriating at worst. The clues would be a *"word salad."* Imagine sitting down to a game of bridge if you have no idea what the rules are. It would be confounding to you and infuriating to your bridge partner. The cards would all seem equally valuable or valueless to you. Such an obviously doomed endeavour would hardly make you happy.

Valuing Process over Product

Flow-inducing experiences tend to be goal-directed, and are bound by a certain set of rules or principles. People who engage in flow activities do so with some sort of plan: they want to accomplish something.

Goals, however, can be short term or long term. And gratification can come sooner, or later. A tennis player who wants to win a tennis match has a short-term goal, as does a mountain climber who wants to reach a summit. But a musician practicing piano may have the long-term goal of improving over time, even if each practice session advances this goal only imperceptibly (at least to an outside observer).

Yet, although flow pursuits tend to ultimately produce results, it's important to note that the end result or product itself is not the cause of the flow. Flow experiences are primarily autotelic experiences. Exhilaration comes from the doing, not from being done.

Autotelic combines two Greek words—auto (self) and telos (goal). An autotelic experience is a self-contained activity that is done not for the sake of future reward or benefit but simply for the joy of doing it. On the other hand, an exotelic experience is one in which the results are of primary importance. If you are singing because you love to sing, you are having an autotelic experience. If you are singing strictly to get on American Idol, you are having an exotelic experience.

People engaged in optimal experience enjoy the process of doing whatever it is they are doing. The gardener in flow loves to turn the soil, to plant, to prune, and to care for his flowers and plants. If his goal is to grow a prize-winning rose, his success will likely make him happy—but not as happy as he was when he was working toward that success. Before you know it, he'll be out in the garden planting again. It is the same for the composer, the painter or the sculptor. After they complete their work, they long to begin the creation process anew. Like children at play, they don't want the game to end, and when it does they want to start another game.

Intensely Focusing Attention

One of the most common attributes cited about the state of flow is that it involves a complete, intense focus of one's attention. Awareness is heightened, but only select information having to do with the task at hand enter into one's moment-to-moment consciousness. Nothing extraneous or irrelevant to the process seems to register.

There are a number of reasons why this type of heightened awareness and intense focus creates a joyous state. During periods of flow, we are not worried. All the *"what-if"* thoughts and anxieties that typically occupy our minds are temporarily kept at bay. They would only be a distraction, and we won't tolerate distractions. If a worry intrudes on a person in flow, it is swatted away like a fly. We are not self-conscious during periods of flow. We are, for a time, able to transcend our preoccupation with our *"image."* What others have thought of us in the past, what kind of reactions we're eliciting in the present, or how we'll be judged in the future are irrelevant. A ballplayer in flow while at the plate is not concerned with cheers or boos. Later on, watching the video replay, he may smile or cringe at how his fans responded to his turn at bat. But while he has his bat in hand, only the game and his role in it exist.

When we're in flow, we lose track of time. Time is our external yardstick for measuring the duration of events. Time is allegedly objective, but we all know that time can subjectively seem to *"drag"* or *"fly."* Minutes can seem like hours when we are bored or filled with dread. But when we are happily in flow, hours can seem like minutes. People in flow often have no idea how much actual clock time they have devoted to their activity. A painter at her easel may tell herself she'll stop work at 8 P.M., only to find herself amazed that it's *"suddenly"* midnight. On the other hand, time in a particularly intense moment of the flow process can seem to be extended, or more accurately— suspended. A basketball player taking a jump shot can perceive these few seconds in something like slow motion, his each mid-air micro-movement etching itself indelibly on his mind. This, too, represents a thrilling departure from our usual temporal reality. The absence of worry, the suspension of self-consciousness, and the subjective reframing of clock time are all results of the intense allocation of attention. Naturally, when the chosen activity ends, consciousness returns to its more mundane mode. However, people who have been in flow have had what could be called a growth experience. They have expanded their concepts of who they are, of how they can feel, and of what is possible. And they are wiser and happier for it.

Finding Time to Flow

Of course, to pursue an activity where one can lose track of time, one first has to make time for it. Unfortunately, this is not the current trend in American society. For decades now, pollsters have been asking respondents in the United States how much time they spend at work and how much time they have available for leisure. And for the past three decades, the clear trend is that we are spending more time at work and less time at leisure. Women, it turns out, have even less time for leisure than men—especially if they have jobs and children. The explanation is that the bulk of child-rearing and housekeeping duties still seemingly fall to women, even in two-parent households. Some fortunate souls are able to earn a living from their flow activities, or at least incorporate some flow activities into their daily work. But anyone else interested in upping their potential for happiness might think about prioritizing *"spare"* time to pursue stimulating activities that offer the opportunity to focus intently and to rise to a challenge.

As for waiting until the day when you don't have to work any longer, studies indicate it's probably not a good idea to take an *"I'll wait until I retire"* approach. Retirees may have more time for leisure and recreation, but tend not to take up new interests after they exit the workforce. It's wiser to develop interests at a younger age and plan to expand your pursuit of them when you retire.

If you find it difficult to devote even one day a week to leisure and play, consider the practice of "Saturday pennies." There are 52 Saturdays in a year and 75 years in the average life span. That means we each are allotted some 3,900 Saturdays. Take your own age, multiply by 52, and subtract that number from 3,900. (For example, if you are 39 years old you have already "spent" 2,028 Saturdays.) Put a penny in a clear glass jar representing every Saturday you have left until age 75. (For a 39-year-old, that's 1,872 pennies.) Every Saturday, take a penny out. As you "spend" your penny stash, ask yourself: have you spent your day in a way that brings you satisfaction? By the way, when you reach 75, put a penny in the jar for every extra Saturday you've been given. And each week, ask yourself what you've done with that gift.

Do You Know Your Flow?

Making space for flow to occur might seem like putting the cart before the horse if you're not sure what your flow activity might be. Some people can pinpoint immediately the activity that allows them to combine play with passion. They'd love to have more time for making jewellery, or practicing the saxophone, or editing videos on their computer. But others may draw a blank. If you are not sure what your potential flow activity is, start by answering the following questions:

- What activities do I enjoy that use my talents and capabilities?

- What subjects do I know a lot about?

- What pursuit do I find challenging and compelling—but never so challenging that I want to give up?

- What is an activity that I like at least as much for its own sake as for what I get out of it?

- Is there something I do where I look at the clock and cannot believe how much time has gone by?

- Is there an activity that I become so engaged in I sometimes even neglect to stop to eat?

- Is there an activity that I enjoy that, for me, has a mildly addictive quality to it?

- Is there an activity or subject that I am always eager to learn more about?

- Is there an activity or subject that I am always eager to talk about with people who do the same thing?

- Is there one pursuit that I always want to get better at?

If you are having trouble identifying a potential flow experience for yourself, try asking yourself what you most enjoyed playing when you were a child? Is there any way you can integrate that into your life as an adult? If you are still having difficulty, don't be afraid to experiment and try different activities on for size.

"When you follow your bliss ... doors will open where you would not have thought there would be doors, and where there wouldn't be a door for anyone else." —Joseph Campbell

If you are on a quest to find your flow, try to let go of any judgments you may have about what is an appropriate choice. Don't steer yourself toward one activity over another because you feel—or someone else feels—that is more highbrow, more suited to your age, or even more suitable for one gender or another. Go with whatever intrigues and engages you.

The following suggestions for starting places are only that: suggestions. Follow your instincts.

Art from the Heart

Making art—drawing, painting, sculpting, potting, and the like—enables many people to experience flow. What's more, artistic endeavours can be both physically and emotionally healing. As we focus completely on an artistic act, studies show heart rate and respiration slow, and blood pressure lowers. But art's healing ability also stems, in part, from the way it can express deep-seated feelings that we might believe is inappropriate to express directly.

The artistic process is also particularly effective in helping us suspend linear thought and objective *"clock time."* As we interact with paints, paper, clay, pen, or pencil, we lose our self-consciousness and, instead, begin to tap the power of our unconscious.

When the project in which we are engaged is complete, we have something to show for it. And even if the end product is not as important as the process, it can be rewarding to have created something—even if we choose not to show it to anyone. If you are intrigued by the idea of creating art but don't know where to begin...

- Try visiting an art museum (move through it slowly and pay close attention) or looking through art books for inspiration.

- Look for other venues that might offer visual inspiration—such as botanical gardens or bird sanctuaries, or even a farmer's market chock-full of lusciously colourful fruits and vegetables.

- Don't worry about buying the best materials—start with the basics.

- Don't be afraid of simplicity—try some fundamental exercises such as drawing basic shapes.

- Don't be afraid of abstraction—art does not have to be a literal re-creation of what already exists.

- Make a space in your home to work (even a small desk or fold-out table) and organize around it the things you will need—so you can slip away during quiet moments and dive right into the process.

Finally, try to think back to a time in your life when you were genuinely excited about making art. You might have to go as far back as kindergarten, because much of our later schooling does not allow a lot of time for original artistic expression. But childlike exuberance is exactly the feeling you are after.

Glory in the Garden

If you know any gardening buffs, you may have witnessed the joy they attain from kneeling on the earth and digging their hands in dirt. They probably were never so happy since making mud pies as children. But it's not the mere physicality of gardening that captivates them. Gardening is also about the joy and satisfaction of nurturing. The gardener's planting and tending brings the beginnings of life to fruition. Their intense, caring focus enables blossoms to grow and thrive. And their labour results in beauty that all can share. Moreover, environmental psychologists believe that spending time in those beautiful, natural surroundings can positively influence our state of mind. So a garden seems like a perfect venue for pursuing a quest for happiness and flow.

Of course, not everyone believes they have the requisite green thumb for this horticultural pursuit. But plants are meant to grow, and even if you've had a bad experience with the odd houseplant here and there, you can probably stage a comeback. If you're just starting, start small. Even if you have more land than the Ponderosa, cordon off a manageable plot. If you live in an apartment and have no outdoor space, you might want to look into the availability of public gardening space—often sponsored by schools, churches, and state-wide environmental organizations. If that's not an option, you can plant a small, simple garden in a window box; just find out which kinds of plants thrive in such quarters.

"Happiness held is the seed; happiness shared is the flower."
—*Anonymous*

Next, find something to plant that is not as temperamental as, say, rare orchids. Some types of flora require more care and feeding than others so visit a nursery and ask for hearty plants that are more or less fool proof. You can also find out about the relative hardiness of various plants by perusing gardening books and magazines—a potentially enriching and diverting pastime in itself.

The Satisfaction of Sports

Many people say they are happiest when they are playing a game of golf, basketball, soccer, softball, or whatever their sport of choice. Whether they realize it or not, if they are playing well against evenly matched opponents and using their skills optimally, they are probably enjoying a state of flow. Time passes without them realizing it, and they are focused intensely on what is happening in the moment.

If you are adept at a sport, or were at some point, consider setting yourself the goal of getting better at it. However, if you consider yourself *"sports challenged,"* don't despair. This condition might also describe several of your friends. If you take up a sport together, you will be evenly matched and can enjoy the process of the game without feeling self-conscious. You'll get a workout, share camaraderie and commiseration, perfect your technique (such as it is)—and laugh! That's a lot of happiness to be mined from one new activity.

The Joy of Being a Beginner

One can be an expert at doing something and, in doing it, create flow. And one has expert knowledge of a field—such as an aficionado of opera, a devotee of foreign films, or a connoisseur of fine wine—that elevates the act of appreciation to a peak experience. But even experts must start somewhere. At a certain point, everyone was a beginner.

Beginners, too, can enter a state of flow as they manifest an attitude of awe and wonder coupled with the excitement of entering unexplored terrain. Allowing yourself to be surprised by new thoughts, new ideas, and new sensory input can help you recall the world as it seemed to you when you were a child—a child who loved to play.

When you begin any new pursuit, don't give in to the urge to over accessorize or overspend. Focus on the process itself rather than the status implied by its accoutrements. Do consider taking some classes. They'll help you with basic techniques, help you build confidence, and allow you to meet others with similar interests.

But when you feel comfortable with the basics, plunge in. If you found something that you enjoy, that's good. If you have found a potential gateway to flow, so much the better. If what you're doing turns out not to be for you, you can chalk any project up to a learning experience—and start something new!

FOURTEEN

Spirituality

"Doing the best at this moment puts you in the best place for the next moment."

Oprah Winfrey

In recent years the biggest media story concerning the human mind and religion has been the lively debate about humanity's genetic predisposition to seek out the divine. Noted scientists have contended that we are all programmed with a so-called *"God gene."* We are neurochemically *"wired,"* they say, to create soothing stories of a benevolent higher power and an eternal afterlife—the better to swallow the bitter pill of our mortality.

Theologians, on the other hand, take a different view of spiritually inclined genes. If we have God-seeking DNA, they say, it is part of a divine plan—a preordained biochemical boost to jump-start us on a journey to unite with the Almighty. This is not a debate likely to come to a definitive resolution. But for practical purposes, that doesn't matter. Because whatever the reasons for human spirituality, spirituality is widely recognized by scientists and theologians alike as generating well-being and happiness.

For thousands of years, human beings have turned, in times of distress and unhappiness, to the person in our community—shaman, monk, rabbi, or mullah—with spiritual credentials. We have sought guidance on how to live a rewarding life from spiritual texts, from the Hindu Vedas to the Koran to the Old and New Testaments. We have searched what we refer to as our souls to summon the hope and strength to rebound from troubling emotional events and cope with physical infirmities. Yet, until recently, neither medicine nor psychology had devoted much study to the effect of spiritual belief and practice on our physical and mental state.

In the United States, two prominent early psychologists expressed interest in certain religious and spiritual phenomena. William James was particularly interested in esoteric elements such as mysticism and trance states. G. Stanly Hall—who actually published a journal devoted to the psychology of religion in the early part of the nineteenth century—was interested in the religious and moral training of young people. But after Hall's journal ceased publication in 1915, religion largely disappeared as a subject of psychological study for several decades. Neither behaviourism, which looked at immediate forms of reinforcement as determinants of human behaviour, nor the Freudian school of thought, which dismissed the longing for God as a displaced longing for an elusive, perfect father figure, gave any credence to what the power of belief could accomplish.

In the 1960s and 1970s, however, things began to change. Publications such as the Journal for the Scientific Study of Religion were founded. Empirical research began to accrue. And in 1975, the American Psychological Association created a division devoted to the psychology of religion.

In the medical field, interest in the power of spiritual belief also burgeoned in the latter part of the twentieth century. After noting the role of religious or spiritual beliefs in helping people counter the debilitating physical effects of stress, modern healers were converted to the idea that something as ethereal as faith could have profound physiological consequences.

Harvard University Medical School, along with similarly prestigious institutions, began holding conferences bringing together renowned physicians and religious scholars. And by 2006, two-thirds of America's medical schools had adopted courses on spirituality and health.

Psychologists, too, were intrigued by all the data showing correlations between spirituality and stress reduction. They began to wonder what other domains were impacted by spirituality and religious practice. Thanks to the influence of positive psychology, there was special interest in the link between individuals' life satisfaction and their sense of connectedness to something beyond their immediate, earthly existence. The data began to accumulate. It shows that religious involvement among adults predicts well-being and happiness. But what, exactly, constitutes religious involvement? Does being spiritual, but not religious per se, "count" in terms of enhancing personal happiness?

Religion and Spirituality: What's the Difference?

If you are one of those who attend religious services weekly, you may well get a happiness boost from doing so. But what if you are someone who believes in some sort of divine force—perhaps with great conviction—yet you do not participate, or participate only minimally, in a formal, organized religion? Will this particular path to happiness elude you? The answer: not at all. You are hardly alone if you consider yourself *"spiritual but not religious."* And you needn't fear that not attending a church, mosque, synagogue, or temple on a regular basis will exclude you from the ranks of the spiritually satisfied.

Many people desire and manifest a divine-oriented element in their lives, although without the traditional religious context. Demographic research shows that the baby boomer generation dropped out of organized religion in unprecedented numbers. But they, along with members of ensuing generations who continue the trend, often say that they did not drop out because they had lost interest in this aspect of life. Rather they were seeking more personal pathways to meet their needs. Being unaffiliated does not mean being unbelieving. Being *"informally"* spiritual is a deep source of satisfaction for millions.

On the other side of the coin, merely going to religious services regularly—without, so to speak, practicing what is preached—is not necessarily a path to happiness. In 1950, Harvard psychologist Gordon Allport (Allport, 1950), one of the few psychologists displaying an interest in the study of religion during that period, made a distinction between what he called extrinsic and intrinsic religiosity. A purely extrinsic orientation means participating in an institutionalized religion strictly because doing so provides approval and status. An intrinsic orientation involves taking the credo of one's religion to heart and striving to bring one's behaviour into harmony with it.

For the purposes of achieving happiness, going through the motions of religion without commitment won't do. The happiness that grows from the spiritual path does not result from outward conformity. Whether you go to church or not, what impacts your happiness is the effect your belief system has on your worldview, your character, and your personal behaviour choices.

Attending worship services does not guarantee a path to happiness, but it certainly does not preclude it. In fact, attending religious services is an excellent means of obtaining social support within your community—which is, in itself, a boon to happiness and well-being. If you are both religiously observant in a formal way and have internalized the teachings of your religion, you may reap the benefits of both orientations.

What Spirituality Offers

Inherent Meaning

Those with a belief in divine power are apt to view the world and their place in it as a coherent system that follows some sort of logical order. Even when things seem incomprehensible on the surface, the faith that sustains believers instils in them the conviction that although they may not understand the grand plan, there is indeed a plan that will unfold exactly as it should.

Acting on the premise that their life has inherent meaning—as opposed to asserting that all events are random—serves to help believers find a sense of purpose that infuses them with energy. They feel connected to something larger than themselves and understand their individual role as one that honours that connection.

"There is enough light for those whose only desire is to see, and enough darkness for those of the opposite disposition."
—Blaise Pascal

Having faith that everything is as it should be and will be as it should be appears not to instil fatalism in believers, but rather to instil optimism. Believers maintain a high degree of faith that everything will work out for the best, and studies show they are less *"thrown"* by potentially traumatic events such as unemployment, divorce, illness, and even the death of a loved one. Their fortitude comes not from denying or ignoring their problems, but rather from accepting them and finding ways to cope with them. In the end, they feel, all will turn out for the best.

However, it does bear mentioning that, as with optimism, religious faith and thoughts of the next life should be tempered with pragmatism and tolerance to generate satisfaction in this life. To generate happiness, faith must derive from sincere devotion, rather than from a desire to control others.

Virtuous Values

Those who internalize the teachings of a particular religion, or of a general spiritual orientation that incorporates the lessons of many religions, tend not only to live more meaningful lives but also more virtuous ones. The virtues they embrace, if put into action, can build and reinforce character strengths that contribute to happiness. Among the virtues extolled by virtually all major religions are the following:

- Compassion

- Gratitude

- Charity

- Honesty

- Tolerance

- Reverence for life

Having a religious orientation does not ensure that one will always act in accordance with such values, but most religions offer clear guidelines meant to help those who stray return to the path of virtue. Codes of behaviour such as those comprised by the Ten Commandments or the Eightfold Path of Buddhism spell out expectations for acceptable behaviour that should result in leading a *"good life."*

If you are uncertain what spiritual direction might hold the most meaning for you, exploring spiritual perspectives through reading can be a satisfying activity itself? You might choose from among traditional scriptures such as the Bible, the Koran. Or you might consider books by contemporary spiritual leaders and commentators, such as the Dalai Lama or Deepak Chopra.

An Attitude of Awe

Believers are also apt to approach the world with a sense of wonder and awe. They are predisposed to seek out and recognize the sacred in the ordinary— from a blade of grass to a starry night. They tend to appreciate nature and to recognize beauty throughout creation.

Spiritual faith can even predispose one to believe in miracles. The idea that anything is possible can be sustaining in one's darkest moments.

Enhanced Self-Care

Finally, those with spiritual beliefs are likely to consider themselves something of a miracle—and therefore worthy of care and tending.

Not surprisingly, spiritual people are less apt to abuse drugs, commit crimes, or commit suicide. Research documents that they are physically healthier and live longer.

Meditating for Happiness

One of the most widespread spiritual practices is the practice of meditation. A far greater number of people meditate on a regular basis than attend religious services on a regular basis.

Nearly all world religions consider some form of spiritual practices a central element of the spiritual life. But can they make us happier? The answer appears to be yes. Some meditation practices specifically address happiness.

And as does this traditional Buddhist meditation on Love and Kindness:

May you be happy, healthy and whole,
May you have love, warmth and affection
May you be protected from harm and free from fear,
May you be alive, engaged and joyful
May you experience inner peace and ease

In fact, many scientific studies have validated the health effects of prayer or meditation. Some researchers speculate this is no miracle per se, but rather a reflection of the effect that prayers-meditations can have on bodily systems by inducing a state of mental tranquillity.

Happy Rituals

Another type of spiritual practice that can add a sense of peace and positivity to our daily lives is weaving some manner of sacred ritual into routine activities. Rituals can encompass a broad range of small and simple activities. But at the same time they can be symbolically profound. They can infuse pleasure into seemingly mundane tasks, and they can also provide us with a greater sense of meaning in our day-to-day lives.

To enhance your daily happiness, consider trying some of these daily spiritual rituals:

- Start each morning by stepping outdoors, breathing deeply, and acknowledging the potential of the new day.

- Begin the day with a series of stretches that celebrate the power and grace of your body and that remind you to stay flexible in attitude.

- Once a day, place a fresh flower on your kitchen counter or dining table-stop momentarily to note its beauty and sweet aroma.

- Transition from work time to home and family time by turning the car radio news off and turning on an inspirational or devotional musical selection.

- Transition to bedtime by turning off the TV and electronic devices.

- End each day by writing in a gratitude journal.

Rituals offer a respite from the ongoing barrage of thoughts, feelings, and worries that continually flow through our busy minds and resonate in our bodies. Rituals anchor us in the present moment, renew and restore us, and nourish our sense of awe. In short they can remind us to be happy.

CHAPTER 4
HAPPINESS AND WORK

FIFTEEN

Do You Like Your Job?

*"Choose a job you love, and you will never have to work
a day in your life."*

Confucius

Work can be a great source of satisfaction—or not. When we're fortunate enough to have work that brings pleasure, meaning, and purpose, our entire life takes on a more positive quality. That's not just because we spend so much time at work, but also because so much of our identity is wrapped up in our work.

Anyone who's ever worked a day knows, too, that work can be a great source of dissatisfaction and of high levels of stress. Of course we can't control everything that happens at work. But, as this chapter explores, to the extent we can control our approach to our work and our attitudes surrounding it, we will be happier on the job, and off.

Doing What You Do Best

A basic explanation of work is that it is something people do to make money. But if money were the only reason to work, then job satisfaction would go up as income goes up. We'd expect to find that the more you make, the happier you are—every lawyer would be happier than every teacher, and every investment banker would be happier than every hairdresser. But such is not necessarily the case. Job satisfaction has many determinants. Among those that figure prominently is that people want to feel they are doing something they are good at.

The Gallup polling organization decided it could learn a lot about how happy people were at work by asking the question, *"Do you get to do what you do best every day?"* But only 20 percent of the thousands of people surveyed answered yes. Those people loved their jobs. The implication is that if more people did what they did best when they were at work, more people would be enthusiastic about working.

After analysing the results of their survey, the Gallup organization concluded that we can get more satisfaction from work by spending more time at work using our most potent skills and strengths. What we do well, we should find ways to do more of. That's a better use of our time than trying to make up for deficits in other areas. For example, if our job involves making client presentations (which we love and are good at) and cold calling prospective clients on the phone (which we loathe and aren't good at), we're better off honing our presentation skills than trying to improve our phone skills.

Finding Flow on the Job

Suppose you are unsure what strengths to cultivate. A good first step in determining which of your skills might make you happier and more successful at work is considering what you do in other areas of your life that puts you into a state of flow. A flow state is one in which you are fully focused and engaged in working to the height of your ability, often to the extent where hours spent on a particular activity can seem like mere minutes. Look especially to areas where you exercise creativity in any manner. Do you like to write, for example? Look for opportunities to write more on the job. At first you might not imagine what writing reports at work might have in common with penning haiku in your spare time. But writing anything at all uses a skill set that involves the selection and ordering of words and the organization of information.

Do you enjoy building things and *"pottering"*? Look for opportunities where you can use this craftiness and inventiveness. Think about what tools or products you use or produce at work. Can you think of ways to improve upon them or use them more efficiently?

To enhance your potential for on-the-job flow, look for areas that you are interested in learning more about. Are these areas of interest applicable to your job? Is there any aspect of your job or industry you would be excited to learn more about? Or do you want to improve upon any of your work-related skills?

Flow is a very personal matter. One man's flow can be another man's phobia. One person might relish the idea of teaching a roomful of sixth-graders because they love the challenge of holding people's attention. Another might have a better time getting a root canal. One person might relish the daily roller coaster ride of an air traffic controller because they love employing spatial skills at a rapid pace. Another person might view such a job as heart attack fodder.

Don't wait for anyone to invite you to learn more. Being creative is partly about creating your own opportunities. Take a class, read a book, sign up for an online course. In this time of fast-paced change, employers reward people who are self-motivated to learn. Today, certain kinds of information can seemingly become obsolete in a heartbeat, but the love of learning itself will never be obsolete.

For most people, the complete elimination of boredom or tedious tasks at work is an unrealistic dream. The trick is to look for positive aspects of the situation to neutralize negative aspects. For example: I don't like filling out forms, but after I do this paperwork I will have the resources to complete my project.

Of course, looking for chances to flow at work is not a license to ignore the parts of a job that are necessary but perhaps not—for you—the most challenging or riveting. In the vast majority of cases, this wouldn't be very pragmatic. If you are a personal trainer who loves training but hates scheduling appointments, you'll quickly run out of clients to train.

However, if we use even 10 percent of our time at work each day exercising our strengths and talents in a way that contributes to flow, we will be ahead of the game, having gone a great way toward increasing our happiness and our effectiveness.

Eyes on the Prize

Using goal-oriented strengths is another way to increase personal satisfaction at work. While flow is about experiencing the joy of the moment, setting satisfying goals is about the positive anticipation of the future. Put another way, flow is about pleasure and meaning. Goals are about purpose.

Goals can be classified as intrinsic or extrinsic. The intrinsic ones have to do with our personal values (I want to make this presentation so engaging that it will be my most effective talk ever). The extrinsic ones have to do with meeting the expectations of others (I have to get these slides done by Tuesday so my boss can approve them before Thursday's meeting).

Meeting intrinsic goals is more likely to result in a sense of happiness and well-being than meeting extrinsic ones. But realistically, any work setting is going to involve meeting other people's goals as well as your own. Your happiness will be enhanced if you can do both at the same time. So, for example, you can make it a goal to organize the best possible presentation you can by Tuesday— and make it so good that your boss won't want to change a thing. Any goal-oriented strength you may possess, such as conscientiousness and perseverance, can be brought to bear on any goal. No matter what you're doing, for example, make a point of doing it expertly and thoroughly, and stick with it until the job is complete. Using your goal-related strengths will be an expression of the values you hold dear, and will also contribute to accomplishment.

Workplace coaches who help their clients increase their success, satisfaction, and enjoyment at work, suggest some strategies when it comes to work-related goals.

The first is to set both short-term and long-term goals. Short-term goals help us continually hone our skills and remind us that we are capable of doing what we set out to do. But long-term goals fuel our hopes and dreams. It can help to use as role models for the latter those who have achieved long-term goals worth waiting for. For example, Walt Disney had the vision of Disneyland when he was a young father accompanying his daughters to what he considered subpar amusement parks. It took him 15 years to bring his dream park to fruition—but 30,000 people visited it on opening day.

Don't over focus on material goals. Again and again, research shows that mere monetary success does not equate to life satisfaction. There's nothing inherently wrong with making money or working toward a goal of getting a bonus, a raise, a promotion—or all three! But people tend to be happier when material success is a by-product of an intrinsic goal, such as creating something innovative or providing a needed service to others.

Don't let passing emotions get in the way of your goals. It's easy to become distracted or unproductive because of anxiety, boredom, or even resentment of someone else's achievements. But drawing on valued character strengths such as personal reliability, commitment to excellence, and internal motivation can stabilize your attitude and get you over the ups and downs of frustrating days. Apply your strengths most to what matters most. Work, being as busy and multifaceted as it is, will often involve meeting numerous goals. With only so many hours in the day, it's necessary to prioritize. Examine the intrinsic and extrinsic value of your goals to determine which one gets the extra push—and when.

Finally, don't let insecurity divert you from your goals. The more goals someone achieves, the more goals they are likely to achieve in the future. To quote Body Shop founder Anita Roddick, "If you ever think you're too small to be effective, you've never been in bed with a mosquito."

People Power

Interpersonal strengths—abilities that have to do with compassion, cooperation, and collaboration—are of paramount importance to people seeking satisfaction in the workplace. Positive and productive work relationships not only help the individuals who cultivate them but help the entire organization create and sustain a more positive culture. Organizational psychologists who specialize in workplace dynamics note that organizations depend not only on the strengths of their individual members for success but also on the strengths of the interactions between workmates, team members, and supervisors and supervisees. High-quality personal connections don't just evolve by chance. They are the outgrowth of attitudes and actions by people who are good at developing and maintaining them.

Friendships That Work

Interpersonal strengths such as empathy, fairness, trust, kindness, loyalty, and genuineness all contribute to an individual's ability to forge and sustain workplace friendships. People strong in social skills have a way of connecting with co-workers. They can readily identify and bond with other individuals who are a *"good fit"* and nurture the relationships in ways that will be mutually beneficial.

Having friends, in general, is a significant contributor to happiness. But friends at work can play a special role. In addition to being a source of encouragement and camaraderie, work friends can be a kind of pressure release valve. When stressors pile up—as they do in even the best work environments—friends can take a break and share a quick laugh or engage in casual banter about anything from sports to shopping. They can also plan to duck out for lunch or get together when the day is done. Brief social forays such as this can make tedious tasks, cranky clients, and similar workplace pitfalls eminently easier to deal with. In fact, engaging in a few minutes of positive social contact is one of the best-known methods of relieving stress.

Friendships at work are more sustainable when they are based on common interests and skills and a shared sense of humour than when they are based on gossip about others or about complaints about *"common enemies."* A continual diet of gripe sessions has been shown to make people angrier, not happier.

Workplace friends who are honest and genuine with one another can also serve as excellent sounding boards. They'll help each other do reality checks. They're a great resource for trying out ideas. And they'll also tell each other if they're overreacting to some minor frustration.

Becoming a Team Player

Whether or not you're officially designated as a member of a team, most work is, in some sense, teamwork. Unless you're a lighthouse keeper, most people's work requires pooling efforts and sharing ideas in a give-and-take process. People with interpersonal strengths are adept when it comes to working collaboratively, even in situations when their teammates are not their friends or their favourite co-workers. There are several ways to sidestep negativity, even in tough situations.

Avoid black-and-white thinking. Few work-related decisions involve choosing between an all-good scenario and an all-bad one. If they did, work would be a piece of cake. Part of being a productive team member is being patient and open-minded enough to look at all the pros and cons, and flexible enough to synthesize solutions based on everyone's input.

Trust the people you work with. Even if you and your co-workers are not *"best friends forever,"* approach your colleagues with an attitude of trust. Unless you have been given repeated, irrefutable evidence that someone is untrustworthy, offer them the benefit of the doubt. Trust is a calculated risk, but if you extend trust with the expectation of success, it will often produce success. Trust breeds trust; mistrust breeds mistrust.

Studies show that low-trust environments lead to low morale and unresolved conflict, not to mention dissatisfied customers. The bad experience for customers in turn has a negative effect on the bottom-line. And the lack of success can contribute to a vicious cycle of even more mistrust. People with interpersonal strengths are good listeners. They listen with careful attention. They are sincerely curious and engaged when someone else is speaking. This sort of active listening gives them a chance to obtain valuable knowledge, and also make the person speaking feel more positively inclined toward the listener. Most of us have an inner radar system of sorts that can tell whether our words are falling on receptive ears or just getting the *"nod treatment."*

Don't jump to conclusions. Often the first response that occurs to us when we are feeling frustrated isn't the wisest or sanest one, or the one most likely to produce positive results. There is a reason why processes such as diplomatic negotiations and labour contract talks take a long time.

People with interpersonal strengths still have very personal emotional responses to events, but they do not let impulsive feelings rule when there is a lot at stake. They allow time for rational thinking to prevail.

They also see the big picture and are willing to sacrifice short-term wins for long-term goals. Resist the temptation to *"yes"* others along and tell them what they want to hear just so they can come up with an easy fix. If your focus is on getting things right, you'll be able to tolerate intermittent uncertainty and even intermittent conflict.

Recognize and acknowledge the efforts and contributions of your colleagues and celebrate their accomplishments. Refrain from grandstanding and always give credit where credit is due.

Be ready and willing to mend fences, not only to forgive but also to ask forgiveness when necessary. If you know how open wounds can fester, you'll take personal responsibility and make amends when you've been at fault.

Keep your sense of humour! People with interpersonal strengths often use humour to bond with others and to ease tension. They know better than to laugh at others or at the expense of others, however. They are especially apt to use self-deprecating humour. They know they won't offend anyone else if they are targeting their own foibles.

Perhaps most importantly, people with interpersonal character strengths refrain from trying to control other people. For one thing, they don't need to control others to feel positive about themselves. For another thing, they tend to be pragmatic. They understand that unless they have a bona fide magic wand, it would be impossible for them to change anyone other than themselves. They are, however, willing to modify their own behaviour to alter the dynamics of their interactions for the better.

Optimism at Work

Having an optimistic disposition goes hand in hand with personal happiness.

But is it a good idea to be optimistic at work? The answer appears to be yes, but with some caveats.

First, for the *"yes"* part. As in other areas of life, research tends to link optimism with increased success on the job. Martin Seligman (Seligman, Authentic Happiness: Using the New Positive Psychology to Realize Your Potential for Lasting Fulfillment, 2002) notes that optimists tend to do better at work than their talents alone would suggest. And management literature abounds with case studies of optimistic leaders who brought their organizations to new heights.

Optimists are more likely to solve problems on the job because they see them as opportunities for bringing about beneficial change. Their desire to achieve positive outcomes, as opposed to the pessimist's desire to avoid negative ones, leads to greater persistence, greater flexibility in strategy, and increased creativity. And, yes, it also leads to more positive outcomes. Certainly optimists can fail, but if they succeed even part of the time, they're ahead of pessimists who never try.

In addition, some business commentators have linked optimism to disastrous business and fiscal policies. The subprime mortgage mess, it has been suggested, was an outgrowth of outrageous optimism on the part of mortgage lenders that housing prices would continue their exponential rise indefinitely. As with almost anything, optimism in the workplace can be taken to unreasonable and unrealistic extremes. It's not hard to see why employees fail to get on board with supervisors who set ill-considered goals and then expect their reports to put in all the effort to meet those goals—while they move on to envisioning even more unrealistic schemes. And it's easy to see how ill-advised policies can be conceived when cock-eyed optimism—tinged with greed—leads professionals who should know better than to refrain from seeking knowledge and to vastly underestimate legitimate risk.

People in the workplace who fly the banner of optimism to justify a lack of accountability give genuine, realistic optimists a bad name. But this is no reason for sincerely optimistic workers to abandon their personal realistic optimism. Realistic optimism is associated with a greater desire to obtain information about how to reach goals and with selection of more attainable aspirations. It's also associated with greater internal motivation rather than pass-the-buck delegation.

The bottom line: if you are a realistic optimist, take your optimistic attitude to work every day. Your upbeat disposition will help you mobilize all your other strengths, will lessen your stress, will help you focus on the most positive elements of your environment, and will help you make meaningful contributions.

If anyone around you seems irritated by your optimism, use your empathic social skills and try to see the world from their vantage point for a minute. It could be they are just not in the mood right now to look on the bright side. Maybe they just need to feel bad for a little while, so they can feel better later. In the meantime, you can have all the optimistic thoughts you like.

How Happy Can Work Make You?

This chapter began by stating that our entire life takes on a more positive quality when we are fortunate enough to have work that brings us pleasure, meaning, and purpose. But just how happy can our work make us?

Work as a Percentage of Life Satisfaction

Research confirms what we might intuitively suspect: that there is a reciprocal influence between job satisfaction and life satisfaction. In other words, satisfaction with one's work tends to make one's life happier overall, and those satisfied with their life overall tend to be happier at work. As in many fields of research, however, investigators disagree about the degree to which job happiness affects life happiness and vice versa.

A study by the Russell Sage Foundation on American quality of life attempted to quantify the relationship. It concluded that work satisfaction accounted for 20 to 25 percent of overall life satisfaction. Although on the face of it this might not seem like a high number, one can appreciate its relative magnitude by considering the many other variables that can impact our happiness—including marital status, social support, health, and so on.

Of course not everyone will have the same proportion of ingredients in their personal happiness recipe.

Job, Career, or Calling?

One factor that could make work more or less significant to someone than the estimated percentage is whether they consider their work a job, a career, or a calling. A study identifying attitudes toward work noted that these are the three primary ways in which individuals in the Western world view what they do for a living:

A job is something one does to earn money. The compensation is of primary interest and the main motivation.

A career is a vocational path with an upward trajectory. The focus is on development, advancement, promotions—in general, on getting to the next level.

A calling is something people feel they were meant to do. Those who see their work as a calling also feel that in doing it they are contributing to the greater good. People who view their work as a calling ascribe the highest degree of meaning to their work. They affiliate it with a higher purpose. And compared to those who see themselves as having jobs, or even careers, they see their work as a great source of joy.

Not everyone may feel they have a calling. That does not mean they cannot be happy at work. People can make friends and use their skills at a job. People can accomplish a great many goals and do a great deal of good in the course of their careers. But even considering what one's calling might be can increase one's potential for happiness.

To do so, return to considering your character strengths and your talents. Ask yourself how you can employ your traits and skills to help others, to further a cause you believe in, or to make the world a better place in some way.

SIXTEEN

Positive Workplace

"Motivation is what gets you started. Habit is what keeps you going."

Jim Rohn

When an organization embodies positive attributes and positive values, that's good for its workforce, good for its customers, and—as savvy business leaders have not failed to notice—good for the bottom-line.

This chapter looks at some key organizational values and examines how they're being put into action to make the workplace more emotionally satisfying and more profitable.

Acknowledging What Goes Right

Organizations typically expend a good deal of effort examining how and why things go wrong. Organizational leaders routinely diagnose problems and search for prescriptive measures to counter them. They ask, *"Why was our forecast off? Why did we not win that contract? Why aren't we getting better recruits?"* It's all an effort to avoid the same problems in the future. This is certainly a sensible approach to self-scrutiny. After all, it would be foolhardy for forward-looking organizations to repeat past mistakes. But in recent years, many progressive organizations have expanded their self-examination to ask, *"What are we doing right?"* And they have initiated efforts to recognize employees who have contributed to their successes. In doing these things, organizations have begun to tap the power of gratitude.

Appreciative Inquiry

Appreciative inquiry (AI) is a positive practice that is becoming increasingly common in businesses, health-care systems, educational institutions, local governments, and religious institutions. It's a method of examining an organization to see what works well and what its life-giving forces (LGFs) consist of. The idea is that every organization must be doing some things right. By identifying those things through appreciative inquiry, its future can be brighter.

Appreciative inquiry uses a four-stage process:

1. Discovery: Identifying the organizational processes that work best.

2. Dreaming: Envisioning of processes that would work well in the future.

3. Design: Planning and prioritizing processes that would work well.

4. Delivery: Implementing the positive processes.

Appreciative inquiry is a highly inclusive process. It is based on the value of equality and acknowledges the importance of community. During the course of the inquiry process, hundreds or even thousands of people involved with the organization in various capacities were asked about their vision of what is positive and what is possible. Ideally, the process itself fosters positive relationships and inspires people to creatively build on the strengths and goodness already in the system.

But appreciative inquiry is as much about unique individuals as it is about the community they form. AI also seeks to discover each person's exceptionality. What are their gifts and their outstanding qualities? The process actively recognizes people for their achievements and for their contributions.

The Power of Praise

In general, today's employers praise their employees more in the belief that positive recognition enhances performance and increases loyalty. Studies show that saying *"thank you"* works. And for those to whom the expression of gratitude at work does not come so easily, there are even management consulting services specifically designed to teach the finer points of praise. In recognition of the positive power of gratitude, many companies have implemented creative praise programs. Some require their managers to write a certain number of praise or thank-you notes to underlings every year.

A caveat when it comes to praise: positive psychologists stipulate that at work, as in school and at home, praise that is baseless, highly exaggerated, or disproportionate will not lead to personal satisfaction nor translate into motivation to develop one's strengths. Praise must be tied to actual achievement to generate happiness and an increased sense of self-efficacy. When praise is earned, the person who earned it will feel that what they've done is significant and meaningful.

Nevertheless, organizations are learning the potency inherent in offering positive feedback for a job genuinely well-done. Even a simple text message that says, "Your presentation was great," can have lasting positive repercussions.

When positive behaviour is recognized, more of the same tends to follow.

Different age groups appear to have different expectations for praise. In some cases, praise has become an intergenerational sticking spot. Some older employees have been reluctant to praise in the workplace because they themselves were not praised for their efforts. As one 60-year-old law firm partner told The Wall Street Journal when he was a young attorney, *"If you weren't getting yelled at, you felt like that was praise."*

Empowering Employees

Trusting employees to evaluate options and make decisions is another practice increasingly favoured by successful organizations. When employees are empowered to make decisions about aspects of their work that directly affect them, they feel a sense of belonging, competence, and control—all of which are highly motivating. In addition, research shows that people feel more positively about any decision that is ultimately made if they believe they have had a voice in it.

Some managers are more inclined to trust than others. According to prevailing leadership theory, whether managers take a participative-democratic approach or a directive *"hand down the edicts"* approach depends on the assumptions they make about human nature. According to this theory, managers can be categorized as either Theory X managers or Theory Y managers:

- Theory X managers assume that workers are lazy, prone to mistakes, and motivated predominantly by money.

- Theory Y managers assume that people are inherently motivated to work for reasons that go beyond financial—for self-fulfilment and because they enjoy satisfying relationships with their co-workers.

In short, Theory Y managers take a more positive view of humanity. They're far more likely to give employees direct control over work procedures and welcome their participation in decision-making. They believe that when employees are given challenges and the discretion to meet those challenges however they see fit, they will demonstrate their competence and their creativity. Theory X managers, as an outgrowth of their assumptions, closely monitor those who report to them. They assign tasks they feel are relatively simple to complete as opposed to those that might pose a challenge. And their idea of incentivizing people begins and ends with the prospect of monetary reward.

The outcomes of these differing attitudes have been clearly demonstrated time and again. Theory Y managers have employees who are more creative and more satisfied. Theory Y is now the guiding force behind the contemporary movement by many organizations to empower employees and to trust the decisions they make.

The Culture of Open Communication

Nowadays one hears a great deal about transparency in organizations. The term connotes an open informational structure in which policies and practices are visible to all interested parties. Transparency in the workplace is in part an outgrowth of technology. Even if those in positions of power wanted to hoard information, it is increasingly difficult to do so, given the ubiquity of online forums, blogs, and chat rooms, not to mention universal and instant electronic access to financial reports.

But for organizations with positive character, transparency is more than a necessary reaction to technology. It is also a proactive philosophy, an outgrowth of a value system that embraces honesty. The more honest and open the communications within an organization, the more trusting employees are—and the better they perform.

Communicating the "Why"

One significant factor in an individual's satisfaction at work is the sense that they are actively working toward some known purpose (other than the pragmatic purpose of getting a pay check). Workers want to know why they are being asked to do what they are being asked to do in the way they are being asked to do it.

In the best-case scenario, employees participate in decisions that impact what they do on a daily basis. Some decisions about larger organizational matters will still inevitably be made at higher levels, but if universal participation in a decision is not feasible, the next best thing is for decision-makers to be forthright not only about what was decided but why.

A study conducted by Phillip G. Clampitt (Clampitt, Phillip, DeKoch, & Robert Transforming, 2010), a consultant and communications professor at the University of Wisconsin at Green Bay, surveyed some 300 managers and employees at more than 100 U.S. employers, asking what they knew of decisions and how supportive they were of them. The study concluded that employees of companies that more fully explained decisions were more than twice as likely to support those decisions as workers who got less information.

Although transparency about motives and rationales behind decisions has been shown to create positive employee attitudes, some executives feel they are too busy to explain their thinking—or that their reasons should be obvious. Nonetheless, time devoted to open discussion of *"why"* is time well spent, because positive attitudes translate to productive performance.

Professor Clampitt (Clampitt, Phillip, DeKoch, & Robert Transforming, 2010) suggests that decision-makers explain new initiatives to workers by telling them...

- How the decision was reached.

- The reasons underlying it.

- What alternatives were considered and rejected.

- How the decision fits into the organisation's overall vision and mission.

- What changes it will mean for the organization.

- How it will directly affect employees.

Satisfaction blossoms when purpose is clear. And the most effective organizations know that honesty about motive and means must not only be genuine, but also specific. To generate positive attitudes and positive outcomes, it's not enough to link a decision to a value in name only. Saying, *"We are changing your compensation to drive innovation,"* or, *"We are reorganizing your department to improve quality,"* is not exactly inspiring. To embrace a united purpose, people want to see how A connects to B.

Keeping Daily Tasks Relevant

In the most effective organizations, honesty from the top also drives interpersonal honesty at every level. On a daily basis, positive, productive employees want to know not only *"why"* but *"how."* How will we be working together? How can what I do each day further the greater goal? When daily tasks seem mindless and meaningless, demoralization sets in.

Management consultants employing a positive-psychology approach believe that, ideally, every direct supervisor in an organization should, within reason, tie daily tasks to the big picture. They should also be honest about the expectations surrounding those tasks: what's needed and when? Nearly everyone in the workplace can tell tales about the boss who repeatedly insisted they needed a particular piece of business on their desk by noon, only to ignore it for days—if they ever acknowledged it at all. These artificial deadlines—essentially a form of crying wolf—have been shown to drive lethargy and apathy. They create undue stress and spark a *"can't do"* attitude. Employees typically approach a falsely urgent task by determining what cannot be accomplished rather than what can.

The bottom line: a lack of transparency about the purpose of tasks and their relative urgency dilutes meaning. Positive organizations attempt to avoid communication patterns that lead to the triumph of the *"urgent"* over the *"important."*

Bad News Beats No News

Creating active engagement can also be facilitated when knowledge is not only shared, but also shared in a timely manner. Research shows that work and work attitudes suffer during periods of extended waiting and uncertainty. Whether it is waiting to learn about key decisions affecting the fate of the organization or waiting for feedback with regard to one's own actions, drawn-out periods devoid of meaningful information lead to boredom, frustration, and rumour mongering.

Studies show that when it comes to an individual's level of happiness, it's apparently better to receive bad news than no news at all. People given bad news can begin to adjust; people facing uncertain outcomes have nothing to adjust to. They may feel paralysed and resist taking any action on any matters whatsoever while their uncertain waiting endures. Or they might do something destructive rather than constructive—simply for the sake of doing anything at all.

Leadership: Character in Motion

The character of an organization depends on its community and its culture. But its leader embodies its character. All leaders lead by example, whether they mean to or not. Leaders set the standards for individuals in their organizations to emulate.

Strengths of Positive Leaders

When leaders are detached, intimidating, or self-serving, their behaviour sends negative emotional messages that take their toll on the organization. Those who work for such bosses say they have learned to be extremely self-protective. They are reluctant to share knowledge or to generate new ideas. According to psychologist Daniel Goleman (Goleman, Emotional intelligence, 1995), an expert in the areas of social and emotional intelligence, leaders with these characteristics can cause "emotional distress that impairs the brain's mechanism to learn and think clearly." But when leaders make a conscious effort to imbue positive values in their organization, those values create a ripple effect. They resonate exponentially, making what's good about the organization even better.

Positive leaders model and in still positive values by...

- Sharing information rather than hoarding it.

- Having transparent motives rather than hidden agendas.

- Empowering individuals to make decisions.

- Communicating clearly about goals and expectations.

- Acknowledging and rewarding achievement.

- Conveying a sense of enthusiasm and optimism.

- Building relationships and conveying a sense of connection.

- Fostering a sense of positive purpose.

None of this is to say, however, that effective leaders coddle those who work for them. As with effective parents and teachers, they don't squander praise and they are not afraid to offer constructive corrections. They know that one of their most important jobs is to continually challenge everyone in their organization to improve.

Reputation and Social Responsibility

Positive leaders also help an organization by enhancing its reputation in the world at large. A company's reputation, the most commonly held perception of an organization's values and character is an intangible but invaluable commodity. A form of psychological capital, it impacts virtually every level of a decision about whether or not people outside the organization want to interact with it: do they want to be its employees, its customers, its business partners, or stakeholders of any kind? That depends on its reputation.

Research shows that a leader who embodies an attitude of altruism is especially effective in boosting an organization's reputation. Social responsibility, as The Wall Street Journal notes, *"is becoming an ever more critical component of corporate reputation."* For example, Microsoft's ascension to the topmost rank in the 2007 Harris Interactive/The Wall Street Journal ranking of the world's best and worst corporate reputations was ascribed to Bill Gates' increasing involvement in his philanthropic foundation.

Most people find it difficult to separate the qualities of leaders from the qualities of their organizations. A socially responsible leader inevitably translates into the perception of an organization as a caring, character-driven entity. Just as an attitude of altruism turns out to be its own reward in private life, where it generates enhanced personal well-being, so it does in public life. In the wider world, altruism not only does genuine good—it also translates into a competitive edge.

Positive Actions in Crisis

Individuals who are positive and character-driven are not immune to crisis, and neither are organizations. In the past, most research on organizational crisis focused on negative outcomes. In crisis, organizations can take positive actions that speed their recovery process and enhance their resilience and overall stability.

Organizational crisis is characterized as *"low probability, high impact"* events. Whether an organization's crisis is externally generated (We sell widgets, but the demand for widgets is down), internally generated (We sell whatzits, but our last batch of whatzits was defective), or caused by multiple overlapping factors (We sell whozits, and our operating costs were already skyrocketing when the hurricane struck), it is the organization's response to the crisis that counts. Facing a challenge or a setback, a positive organization will mobilize its strengths. Good communicators will become better communicators, working to offer transparency as opposed to hiding behind closed doors and keeping the rank and file waiting and guessing.

Creative solutions will be solicited and logically considered. Flexibility will be paramount. In a crisis, positive leaders will lead—as opposed to doubting their abilities or pointing fingers. They will not waste time or energy denying the existence of problems or shirking responsibility. Their commitment will be to get the organization back on track by doing the best thing and right thing.

In the aftermath of a crisis, an organization can flourish. Among the benefits it may reap are the following:

- Heightened attention to its relationships with all of its stakeholders

- Deeper organizational identity

- Increased mindfulness of vulnerabilities

- Enhanced reputation

- Enhanced sensitivity to the emotional needs of its members

Although some organizations are inclined to sweep a bygone crisis under the carpet, others—even while resuming standard operating procedures—take pride in their battle scars. Having faced adversity and survived with dignity, such organizations, and the many individuals that comprise them, know they are better prepared for future challenges—and future success.

SEVENTEEN

Happiness at work

"You can teach a student a lesson for a day; but if you can teach him to learn by creating curiosity, he will continue the learning process as long as he lives."

Clay P. Bedford

Many organizations are doing a great deal to promote a sense of meaning and purpose among their employees. But let's not forget that happiness is also about *"the pleasant life."* As this chapter shows, organizations have a far greater chance of keeping their employees happy—and keeping them around—by making the workplace more flexible and more fun.

Happy Life, Balanced Life

One of the main reasons organizations are invested in employee satisfaction is that they want their workforce to stick around. A happy employee is a loyal employee—and a loyal employee is good for the bottom line. In many industries, it costs a company one and a half times an employee's yearly salary to replace them.

In addition to being loyal, happy employees are willing to go the extra mile. They are willing to help co-workers, ready to take initiative, and eager to promote the company outside of work. All this adds up to what human resource professionals call employee engagement.

In recent years, an increasing number of employers have been surveying workers in an attempt to find out what would make them happier and more "engaged" on a daily basis. Responses show that in addition to wanting work that employs their strengths and managers who respect their opinions, employees want one other key thing: they want their employer to acknowledge that employees have a life outside of work, and they want job flexibility that enables them to enjoy that life. When employers do this, they contribute to their employees' perceived organizational support (POS), an important metric when it comes to measuring work-related happiness.

Employee engagement is the degree to which employees feel pride in their organizations, are loyal to them, and feel they are an important and respected part of them. Perceived organizational support (POS), an important determinant of employees' well-being and satisfaction in organizations, is a measure of how well employees feel organizations assist them in moderating the negative effect of stressors in the workplace.

An interweaving of work life with outside-of-work life is, according to Harvard socio-biologist Edward O. Wilson, not a radical new concept but a natural arrangement for humankind. For most of history, work and family life were intertwined. Hunting and gathering, farming, and craft skills were passed from one generation to the next. The way many people work today—out the door before breakfast, home for a late dinner—dates back to the nineteenth century's Industrial Revolution, when we switched from home-based manufacturing to factory work.

Now employees want that dawn-to-dusk model re-examined. And many companies are obliging by offering various options, including the following:

- Telecommuting, in which employees work from home or a close-to-home satellite office for some of their dedicated work hours.

- Flexi time, in which full-time employees are able to craft their own daily schedule (although they are sometimes required to work onsite for certain "core hours").

- Compressed workweeks, which allow employees to condense a 40-hour work week into fewer than five days.

- Permanent part time, in which employees, up to and including high-level managers, work less than a 40-hour week.

- Job sharing, in which two part-time employees share responsibility for one job that requires full-time coverage.

Each of these options provides employees with increased discretionary time to spend with friends and family or pursuing hobbies and recreational activities.

Because all of these have been shown to increase happiness, employees who avail themselves of such opportunities are likely to report for work with a better mood and attitude. They're also apt to be less drained from one of the greatest happiness-sappers of our time: the daily commute.

Commuting: The Happiness Crusher

Sometimes it is the seemingly little things in life that make us happy, or unhappy. Most of us don't think of commuting as a significant aspect of our existence. It's just an *"in-between"* time when nothing much happens. Yet a growing body of evidence shows incontrovertibly that people with long journeys to and from work report having significantly lower subjective well-being. Their unhappiness has to do not only with what happens during their daily travel time, but what does not happen.

The Paradox of Commuting

People consistently rank commuting as one of the unhappiest times of their day, yet many people accept longer commutes to jobs farther away if the jobs offer more money or if they can afford a bigger house in a more distant locale. Apparently, this is a faulty strategy as far as personal happiness is concerned. Two economists at the University of Zurich, Bruno Frey and Alois Stutzer, released a study called *"Stress That Doesn't Pay: The Commuting Paradox."* They found that someone whose commute is an hour each way would have to make 40 percent more in salary to be as *"satisfied"* with life as a non-commuter is. Most are far from adequately compensated.

Why does commuting make people so miserable? Because it is unpredictable, for one thing. Humans have a way of adapting to stressors—even very serious ones, such as accommodating a physical handicap. When the adaptation is complete, our happiness level reverts to where it was before. But, as any commuter can attest, it is virtually impossible to predict with certainty how long a supposed one-hour commute will actually take. Accidents, bad weather, road construction, politicians' motorcades, and countless other random and uncontrollable factors can prolong behind-the-wheel angst—with no way to tell, while actually sitting in traffic, when it will end. Every time commuters get into the driver's seat, they are playing a game of chance with a potentially negative outcome—similar to Russian roulette. But there is another major reason why commuting is so hard on people.

According to Frey and Stutzer, and others who have studied the problem, commuting takes an enormous toll on happiness because the time devoted to this activity cannot be devoted to happiness-promoting activities—such as exercise, sleep, and socializing.

Robert Putnam, a Harvard political scientist, calls commuting *"a robust predictor of social isolation,"* and notes that social isolation directly causes unhappiness. Putnam has even quantified the negative; every 10 minutes of commuting, he says, result in 10 per cent fewer social connections. Putnam advises each person who will potentially commute to work to visualize a triangle comprising where they sleep, where they work, and where they shop and socialize. In many cities, you can spend an hour or two traveling along each side of that triangle. However, the smaller the triangle, the happier the person. The happiest people of all would be able to walk everywhere.

Easing Commuting Pain

With commuting creating unhappy consequences for workers and for the environment, and with globalization creating a need for varied employee availability, it's likely that even resistant organizations may become increasingly inspired to offer more flexible work arrangements. Until then, not everyone will be able shrink their commuting triangle. Nevertheless, commuters can take some actions to lessen commuting stress. If you're among the unhappy commuting cadre:

- Get ready the night before. Lay out clothes and briefcases and even pack your lunch at night. It can buy you time in the morning to have a few quality family moments, not to mention a nutritious breakfast.

- Stock your car with entertainment—and knowledge. Order audio versions of all the books you've wanted to read. Keep your favourite music CDs on hand as well, so you will never lack for entertainment.

- To add greater purpose to your travel time, consider learning a new language—or brushing up on your high school French while you're in automobile.

- Work out after work. If your boss won't flex your schedule, flex it yourself —along with your muscles. Join a gym near work and spend some time there in the evening before hitting the road. The time you spend on the treadmill should cut the time you spend in traffic if you have been habitually leaving at rush hour.

- Change your routine now and again. To keep boredom at bay, vary your route or, better yet, vary your method of commuting. Try public transportation or, if at all possible, see if you can bicycle on a fine day.

- Ride with a friend. Because this eases social isolation, it is perhaps the best way to diminish commuting's anti-happiness effects. Studies show that ride sharing lowers commuter stress significantly, and also that it is easier to relax while someone else does the driving.

Finally, anyone faced with an arduous commute should be certain to get a good night's sleep to restore body, mind, and mood. If their employer is one of the growing number who are providing time and space for naps at work, they should take advantage of the perk-preferably sometime between the hours of 1 and 3 P.M., when research shows that most of us could use a biological boost. Adequate sleep not only decreases the likelihood of flaring tempers and road rage, but also promotes safety behind the wheel. That's good, because nothing compounds the unhappiness of commuting like a car accident.

Having Fun on the Job

When it comes to keeping employees around, keeping them happy, and keeping their relationships with one another on a positive note, effective organizations have another strategy up their sleeves. It does not necessarily require a lot of money; nevertheless, it does require time, thought, and attention. It is—simply enough—making sure employees have more fun on the job.

When Fun Works

Some people think of *"work"* and *"fun"* as antithetical concepts (and it's a pretty sure bet that those people aren't happy at work). Lots of other people think of fun on the job as something that happens only *"accidentally"*—for example, a spontaneous outburst of laughter that relieves tension but is quickly suppressed to avoid drawing a supervisor's attention. Still others think of fun on the job as something they can only have with their good friends—so they grab lunch and swap stories in small groups.

But recently, many organizations have begun to intentionally create opportunities for employees to play and have fun at work. Proponents of systemized fun say that a little fun doesn't hurt—and, in fact, really helps to up the level of retention. People bond when they have fun together, and want to stay on a job when they are close to their colleagues.

Moreover, fun at work also helps people to take breaks, relieve stress, and even become more creative. As anyone who's ever tried to tackle a knotty problem can attest, it's often easier to view a challenge with a fresh perspective and a burst of energy after a little rest and recreation.

Employers can also attest that fun, in addition to bolstering individual happiness, is a good team builder and a catalyst for company pride. As for customer relations, employees are more likely to provide service with a smile when their smiles are genuine.

There are some caveats, however, to attempting to inject fun into the work environment. Psychologists and management consultants who specialize in the matter (yes, fun consulting is becoming something of a specialty) caution that employers should think about what their staff might actually consider to be fun. One man's fun—be it square dancing, squash, or Scrabble—might be another man's full-blown misery. It's a good idea to find out what employees typically do for fun in their free time and then take cues from those preferences. Fun at work also works best when people at all levels of the organizational hierarchy participate. Enjoyable events won't be enjoyable if they're seen as an indulgence for the *"little people."* Employees take their emotional and behavioural cues from leaders. When leaders loosen up, they do as well. Finally, it's important to remember that planning a game or party is not a cure-all for a dysfunctional environment. Any change, even for the better, takes some getting used to. People need to be given the message that it's safe to have fun, and that the fun represents a sincere commitment to building morale and creating an organization that not only likes to celebrate itself but is worthy of doing so.

Some Fun Ideas

At a New York ad-sales company where most employees are recent college graduates, the sales force participates in group activities with a competitive element—such as city-wide scavenger hunts organized by a team-building and adventure company. At a Columbus, Ohio, industrial-design firm, designers compete against other firms in an annual miniature derby car race, often tinkering with their own automotive entries on a practice racetrack prominently installed in their office. And at a Chicago recruiting firm, employees periodically attend concerts outside the office, and even have performers come in to serenade them.

These are just some of the creative events that organizations have come up with to spread fun and good cheer. Others include the following:

- Paper airplane tournaments

- Company T-shirt design contests

- Crossword puzzle competitions

- Weekly lunchtime pizza parties

- *"Silly hat"* or *"horrid tie"* contests

- "Guess whose baby picture?" (or high school yearbook picture) bulletin boards

- Anniversary parties celebrating employees' "hire days"

An annual holiday office party can seem like an awkward affair if it's the only *"fun event"* of the year, and it can make employees more socially anxious than happy. It's best to spread fun at work throughout the seasons. If holiday parties, or any festivities, include groups of employees who barely know each other, it's a good idea to plan ice-breaker games.

Finally, although it's great to have fun during the good times, it's also important for organizations not to lose their sense of humour or their ability to have fun during the less-than-perfect times. During the down times people most need to feel supported. If *"pizza Wednesday"* is eliminated at the first sign of a lackluster financial quarter, employees will feel punished. If the camaraderie persists, they will remember the many positive reasons why they actually like getting out of bed and going to work each day.

When Happiness Means Saying No to Work

This chapter began by discussing the importance of work-life balance in a happy life. But employers are not the only ones responsible for creating that balance. Employees are responsible, too.

Regardless of how much we enjoy our work and our work colleagues, it's important to know when to stop working.

Knowing When to Quit

Ironically, if work and other parts of life can't peacefully coexist, then all of them—including work —will suffer. It used to be that only a select few of us could properly be labelled *"workaholics."*

It was said that workaholics chose to work all or much of the time to keep from dwelling on unwanted emotions or to avoid intimacy in relationships. Workaholic-type addiction certainly still exists today. Those who have it would likely exhibit extreme signs of work addiction:

- Talking about work a vast majority of the time

- Having friends and family who've given up expecting them at important events

- Working during meals

- Taking work to bed

- Becoming irritable when people ask them to stop working

- Becoming impatient with people who don't work as hard as they do

- Taking on the work of others in the belief that no one else can ever do it as well as they can

However, workaholism is not the main thing that keeps a great many of us tethered to work more or less around the clock nowadays. For that we can thank—or curse—technology that makes us continually accessible, a global economy and global financial markets, and round-the-clock Internet commerce. All these things drive expectations—our own and other people's—that we need to be on the job, or at least on call, 24/7.

But if we are to maintain a happy balance, there are times when we have to be unavailable. Sometimes we have to say *"no,"* or at least *"not now."*

Whatever our work is, and even if we like it enormously, we must trust that we know it well enough to discriminate between which matters need instant attention, which ones can wait, and which ones should wait because they will benefit from some more time and consideration.

If the Thrill Is Gone

Everyone has an optimum work pace that feels appropriate. It is one where they can accomplish a lot and be creative and productive without crossing that fine line into unbalanced burnout. It's important to know when enough is enough. And the tip-off may be that work you once really loved to do now will feel like a grim habit. When the thrill is gone from work, you may just need to do less work to get it back. It's not always easy to slow down, but these strategies can help:

- Continually re-evaluate your "to-do" list. Delete any task that has been on the list more than a week or month with no progress. You are probably not going to do it, so don't let it haunt you.

- Set time and space boundaries. For example, have an e-mail cut-off time when you arrive at home. Pledge to turn off your cell phone (yes, the vibrator, too) during dinner. Announce your intention to be off-line in a nicely phrased automated e-mail reply and cell phone message.

- Shut the home office door. If you work in a home office, you are theoretically able to spend more time with loved ones—but do you? Don't forget to come out of that office at a regular time, and turn off the light and the computer. It will all be there in the morning.

- Take your vacation time. Count the days you have coming and plan to take them off. If you're afraid of pressure build-up while you're gone, take long weekends before building up to weeks.

- Forget the multi-tasking myth. Studies show we are actually most effective when we do one thing at a time. Besides, you'll never get into a flow state unless you focus. (To this end, try turning off your e-mail alert "ping." Check your e-mail at times of your choosing.)

- Ask for help. Use your network. Tap into the expertise of colleagues and co-workers. (Let them know you'll do the same for them.)

- Prepare for peak cycles. Many occupations have their busiest seasons. Short of changing professions, there is nothing to do to prevent a busy season, so spend the months beforehand making sure that your mind and body are in the soundest possible shape. Eating right, getting enough rest and exercise, and tending to your social and spiritual needs will enable you to create a reservoir of energy to draw on when the going gets tough.

Finally, hold on to your long-term goals. Remember the meaning and purpose of what you are trying to accomplish.

Then ask yourself what you can do to put the fun back into your fundamental vision.

CHAPTER 5
HAPPINESS TIPS

EIGHTEEN

The Importance of Exercising

"All truly great thoughts are conceived while walking."

Friedrich Nietzsche

When we think about how to be happy, we tend to think of psychological, social, and even spiritual pathways. But science, medicine, and psychology all agree that a profound mind-body connection exists, and what happens on the physical plane resonates in the psychological arena.

We can undertake physical activities that have a proven impact in creating a positive frame of mind. A landslide of research shows that getting regular exercise is among the best things we can do for our body and will up our happiness quotient. Exercise works so well to improve mood and outlook that many find it, in effect, a golden ticket to happiness.

Active Body, Happy Mind

Unless you've been living under a rock for the past 30 years, you probably know that exercise is good for your body. It can lower blood pressure, strengthen the heart, increase lung capacity, regulate blood sugar, maintain strong bones, increase muscle strength and suppleness, and increase the functioning of our immune system—to name just some of its many benefits. But fewer of us are aware that exercise can also provide a significant psychological *"lift,"* not only in the short term but also the long term.

Exercise and the Well-Lived Life

It's easy to see how exercise can contribute to the kind of happiness that we call the pleasant life. But it can contribute to the good life and the meaningful life as well.

In addition to giving us a physiological mood boost, exercise can give us a mental edge. For one thing, it actually helps create new brain cells—the better to stay alert, alive, curious, and creative. For another thing, exercise tends to instil what is known as *"the mastery effect,"* engendering a sense of personal achievement as we master new skills or get better at old ones. The resulting self-confidence inspires us to tackle new challenges and seek new opportunities. Exercise can also promote more social interaction, which in itself can promote happiness. Joining a gym or participating in a dance class or a running or hiking group means finding potential friends with similar interests. (Not to mention creating a social-reinforcement network that will make it harder to make excuses for not showing up.)

Not a joiner? That might change after you begin shaping up. Exercise not only makes us feel and look better, but also makes us feel better about the way we look. Armed with a trimmed-down waistline, glowing skin, and the enhanced self-image such improvements can instigate, exercisers might find they are more interested than ever in becoming part of a group.

Moving Toward Movement

Getting started with a fitness program need not be a complicated or costly affair. There are usually more mental hurdles than logistical or financial ones. But all hurdles can be overcome in the name of happiness.

Simple First Steps

It doesn't take much more than a comfortable pair of shoes and a little determination to get started on a walking program. You can enjoy the outdoors, say hello to your neighbours (racking up some additional social contact), and vary your route to avoid boredom.

If there's a bicycle gathering dust in your garage, check the air in the tires and spray the gears with some oil. Then find your helmet, or buy a new one, and pedal away to instantly experience some of the fun and freedom you felt in childhood when you were independently mobile. Remember, this is not the Tour de France, so you needn't seek out the highest hill in town. Pick a destination that's a quarter of an hour away, get there, turn around and come back. Next time you can go further if you like.

Swimming promotes strength, stamina, and mobility along with cardiovascular fitness—and immersion in water can have a soothing effect. Access to a swimming pool is probably more readily available than you think. Call your local "Y" or municipal pool and inquire.

Moving Beyond Excuses

Now that you know you don't have to spend a fortune to exercise, what other excuses do you have? Not enough time? Exercise is boring? No companion to work out with? Too embarrassed about the shape you're in now? Most people who have not yet been bitten by the exercise bug can come up with lots of these. But—as with all things—for every negative reaction, there is a positive response:

"Not enough time." Fair enough. If necessary, combine exercise with another activity you do daily. If, for example, you watch a half hour of financial news on television each morning, consider doing so while you walk on a treadmill. Alternatively, consider swapping exercise for an activity that brings you little joy. Perhaps you can bike to the office and avoid sitting in traffic. Finally, consider that regular exercise adds an average of two years to your life. You get all the time spent exercising back in the end.

"Exercise is boring." Not all exercise regimes are for all people. The trick is to find some things you like to do, then mix those things up. Altering your exercise regime prevents monotony and gooses the endorphins again. From time to time, vary your intensity, cross train, take up a new sport, or sign up for a few sessions with a trainer. Keeping your exercise fresh is as important as keeping your love life fresh.

"No companion." After you start exercising you'll likely run (perhaps literally) into others who do the same thing at the same time. It's a great opportunity to "buddy up." However, if you want to leave nothing to chance, sign up for a class or join a gym and fraternize with other workout devotees or fellow novices. Find a gym with convenient hours and a nearby location so you do not generate additional excuses.

"Embarrassed about my shape." Not working out because you are embarrassed about not being in shape is like not going to the dentist because you are embarrassed about having a cavity. You have to start somewhere! Having said that, it's reasonable to avoid situations where you will be thrown in the company of only hard core veterans or exercisers with *"attitude."* Look for a venue that clearly welcomes people at all levels of fitness. If you're self-conscious about your body in front of the opposite sex, consider joining a gym that is gender-specific.

Some people work so hard at coming up with excuses they'd actually expend less effort exercising than stalling. If you count yourself among this number, it's time to stop moving your lips and try putting one foot in front of the other. You'll undoubtedly be happy you did.

Yoga: Thousands of Years of Happiness Training

The practice of hatha yoga, an exercise discipline that has thrived around the world for thousands of years, can also be a way of moving toward happiness. The foundational texts of yoga refer repeatedly to the cultivation of bliss. Contemporary research backs up the yoga-happiness connection.

Yoga, from a Sanskrit word referring to the binding of opposites, is actually comprised of eight interrelated practices, some of which have to do with purifying the body and some with purifying the mind.

Hatha yoga is the aspect of yoga that focuses on physical postures, and here in the West is the typical entry point to yoga practice. Ha means *"sun"* and that means *"moon"*— thus, the word itself incorporates the concept of natural balance.

The Yogic State: More Than Poses

Of course hatha yoga does have many positive effects like the following:

It induces better breathing. While holding each posture, practitioners are taught to lengthen their stretches by deep, slow breathing. This is the sort of breathing that naturally counters stress and tension as it stimulates the body's natural relaxation response.

It engenders increased flexibility, agility, and balance. Even those who consider themselves *"klutzes"* often report feeling more graceful and more in control of their bodies after they take up yoga. This can lead to an enhanced self-image and even to a greater self-confidence at other physical activities.

It can lead to sounder sleeping. Getting enough good-quality sleep is an integral part of overall happiness. Many who have taken up yoga report that it has become easier for them to fall asleep and that they sleep more soundly. Some contend they can substitute 30 to 60 minutes of yoga for 30 to 60 minutes of sleep and feel even better.

It increases focus and present-moment awareness. The practice of yoga does not require a great deal of physical strength or know-how from the beginner, but it does require focus. The postures—called asanas—can be held comfortably for increasing lengths of time as one make progress, provided you keep your mind on the activity at hand. This kind of mindfulness—and the corresponding freedom from the nagging chatter of anxious thoughts—are conducive to creating a sense of contentment and inner peace.

Finally, the long-term effects of yoga practice can include a decrease in self-judgment and self-criticism. Good teachers encourage their students to honour and value their bodies and to respect their current limitations as they gently progress to doing more. With the proper guidance, students can take this positive attitude with them and apply it outside the yoga studio as well.

First Steps on the Yogic Path

If you have never attempted yoga, it might seem as though it is a strange ritual of twisting yourself into a pretzel, perhaps in a semi-darkened room, perhaps with some Eastern-style music in the background. Can this sort of thing really make you happier if the very idea makes you uncomfortable? Is it really for you? As with anything, you will never know until you give it a try. That said, it is true that newcomers to yoga can be intimidated if they don't keep a few things in mind.

Don't be put off by any glossy magazine covers featuring Hollywood stars doing their daily yoga routines or flawless models performing gravity-defying backbends. Everyone has to start somewhere and you can be sure this is not how they started. Even if you never come close to achieving such feats, you can still do yoga and get a great deal out of it.

Also, don't worry that, *"I can't do yoga because I'm not flexible."* That is just like worrying, *"I can't get in shape because I'm not in shape."* Bit by bit, yoga will limber and strengthen you, and you'll start stretching not only your body but also your confidence.

Yoga's Not a Competitive Sport

Perhaps the most important thing to remember about yoga is that it's not a competition. Don't overdo it in the beginning in the attempt to keep up with fellow practitioners. In fact, don't overdo it ever. Your body can have a different tolerance for various postures on various days. It's not about forcing but rather about expanding.

If you find yourself in a class that you feel is too advanced for you, look for a class with a greater number of beginners. There you will receive more detailed step-by-step instruction and, most likely, feel less self-conscious.

Also, be aware that there are many different styles of practice that fall under the general umbrella of hatha yoga. All offer physical benefits as well as the potential to simultaneously relax and energize you. But some take a more vigorous approach, whereas others are slower and more meditative.

After you take a number of yoga classes, you might choose to bring some aspects of your yoga home. Many practitioners put together a personal practice and they take about 20 minutes to do it on a daily basis, wherever they are. Yoga is extremely portable. If you've got your body and a floor, you can do it.

The Effect of Positive Posture

Even if there is no chance of your fitting aerobic exercise or yoga into your life, there is one thing you can do physically that will take but a moment and will change your outlook significantly: straighten up.

Your mother may have always told you to stand up straight, but chances are she did so in order for you to look good. What she probably did not know, but the field of embodied cognitive science has now discovered, is that standing tall can also help you maintain a positive attitude. According to the principles of embodied cognition, manipulating one's stance can causally affect how emotional information is processed.

In one study, participants were divided into two groups: one adopted a posture in which the head and shoulders slumped; the other adopted a posture in which the shoulders were held back and high. Both groups were informed they had been successful on an achievement test completed earlier. Those who received the good news while in a slumped posture reported feeling less proud and being in a worse mood than did those who were standing tall. The subjects with good posture literally embodied happiness.

As long as you're standing up straight, you can take your mother's other classic piece of advice and put a smile on your face. Even when you don't feel like smiling, studies show that forming a grin can lift your spirits and make you perceive communications from others as more positive. If you need help raising the corners of your mouth, try holding a pencil between your teeth.

NINETEEN

The Importance of Sleep

"A well spent day brings happy sleep."

Leonardo da Vinci

Imagine that, on a given day, you've done everything you can, base on what you know, to go to bed happy. You spent part of the day using your strengths at work and in your personal life. You spent quality time with friends and family. You shared a good laugh, did a good deed, and had a good workout. You even took a few moments before bedtime to be consciously grateful for all the positive things in your life. But then it happens: you just can't sleep. Maybe you're tossing and turning because of noise; maybe it's because of a late-night cappuccino you enjoyed; maybe it's because there's something on your mind. Whatever the reason, one thing is for certain: you won't start the next day in an especially happy frame of mind, nor feel well-equipped to continue to do the things that you know keep you satisfied, unless you've gotten a good night's sleep.

The Sleep/Happiness Connection

Getting consistent high-quality sleep is strongly correlated to being happy and productive and feeling emotionally and mentally healthy.

At first this might seem odd. Why should eight hours of *"nothingness"* have such an impact one way or the other? But it makes sense if we really look at what, exactly, sleep is for. It is, in fact, not for nothing.

On a physical level, sleep restores bodily energy supplies that have been depleted during the course of the day. Sleep is also the time when our body repairs muscle tissue by secreting a human growth hormone, which our tissues require even after we are "grown." Sleep improves muscle tone, enabling us to run faster, jump higher, and in general, be agile rather than slow and clumsy. Sleep also appears to boost the body's immune system and helps prevent us from being sick.

On a cognitive level, sleep recharges our mental batteries and keeps the mind sharp. Although the adult human brain accounts for only 3 per cent of body weight, it consumes 25 per cent of body energy. Thinking, creating, and problem solving require lots of "juice," provided by a molecule called glycogen. The slow, steady brain waves of sleep restock our glycogen stores. Some sleep experts also believe that sleep detoxifies the brain by lowering its temperature. And although the jury is still out in terms of the exact purpose of dreams, there is no doubt that the REM (rapid eye movement) stage of sleep that indicates dreaming is essential for optimal mental functioning. Keep us from our

REM sleep, and we can quickly go to pieces under the slightest pressure.

Another reason we feel less emotionally stable with diminished sleep is that restorative, slow-wave sleep (not the REM type, but the type in which we spend most of our sleep time) decreases the amount of stress hormones in our system. A poor night's sleep, let alone several in a row, actually increases the levels of such hormones. Now, little irritants and setbacks that might not ordinarily bother us (especially if we've resolved to keep an optimistic outlook and remember our sense of humour) can suddenly seem overwhelming. In short, a sleep-deprived person will greet each day with a fatigued body, a fuzzy mind, and a propensity for negative emotional overreaction—three clear happiness handicaps. Physical pleasures will seem dulled, making the pleasant life elusive. Mental tasks will feel harder, making it harder to stretch and challenge ourselves in ways that offer personal satisfaction. As for interpersonal relations, they're bound to suffer casualties. It's hard to feel loving, compassionate, or altruistic when we're in a perennial state of crankiness. Instead of lending a helping hand to those in need, we'd be more likely to bite their heads off.

Cutting into Our Happiness

How much sleep is optimal for a happy life? To some extent, that varies from one individual to another. Factors such as physical size, muscle mass, and other variables that affect metabolic rate can vary. But on the whole, if you're in the seven- to eight-hour range, you're in the ballpark.

For much of human history, worrying about how much sleep we got was not an issue. We simply slept when it was dark. With the advent of artificial light, we had more options.

Sleep experts say we make excuses to rationalize our lack of sleep. We say...

- We are exceptions who can *"handle"* lack of sleep.

- Life's too short and we don't want to "waste time" sleeping.

- We're too busy and too in-demand.

- We're not sleepy.

- We'll catch up on sleep later.

But these excuses don't hold up. No one performs up to their potential when they don't get enough rest. The life we are trying to squeeze more actually becomes less rewarding. And all those commitments we think we should keep are actually harder to keep as we lose our energy and focus. As for those who are *"not sleepy,"* chances are they're tanked up on caffeine or sugar, or both. And as for those who say they'll catch up, they're probably fooling themselves. If you need eight hours of sleep and you sleep for five hours, three nights a week, you'd have to spend nine additional hours sleeping during the weekend to catch up. In other words, you'd have to lose most of one waking day. And that's certainly not a happy prospect.

Secrets of Happy Sleeping

The bottom line is that anyone who is not getting enough sleep is not getting the most out of life, no matter what they think. To up our capacity for happiness, we have to take the time to refuel. Sadly, however, some of us have developed some very counterproductive sleep habits and need to teach ourselves to sleep again.

A Serene Sleep Space

If you want to embark on a worthy project, acknowledging your ongoing quest for happiness, consider re-creating your bedroom into a simple space designed for sleeping and not too much else (okay, one other bed-related activity—but that adds to happiness as well). If you have a computer in your bedroom, you will be tempted to work, answer e- mails, do some online shopping, or engage in myriad web-entangling experiences. Because cyberspace never sleeps, neither will you. If you have a television in the bedroom, you'll watch it... and watch it. But although watching TV seems like a passive activity, it is actually stimulating. You'll stay up later than you otherwise might, and when you do fall asleep, the TV might still be blaring. If so, the quality of your slumber will be poorer than it ought to be. Of course, there are things you should have in your sleep space. One of those is a firm mattress—the better to support your spine. The mattress should be big enough to spread out on, but not so big you feel lost. If you like touching your partner during sleep for a reassuring sense of *"home base,"* a full or queen size might suit you better than a king (but the reverse is true if your partner routinely wakes you by tossing, turning, flailing, or inadvertently kicking you in the shins). Keep your bed free of clutter. Rolling over into a crackly newspaper or a crunchy bag of chips can lead to a rude awakening.

Money can't buy happiness per se, but splurging a little might enhance your sleep experience. If you want to feel like you're sleeping on a cloud, invest in a fluffy goose-down comforter. Many sleepers grow so fond of their personalized pillows that they pack them when they travel. Another way you should tend to your sleep space is to keep it at the proper temperature. To facilitate sleep, the bedroom should be between 60 and 65 degrees. If it feels a bit chilly before you get under the covers, you're doing it right. You can always adjust your own temperature after you're in bed by adding blankets or wearing cosy long silk underwear. Keep the room well-ventilated with an open window or two—unless doing so creates a noise factor.

It's also wise to keep the lights in your bedroom low—especially for half an hour to an hour before you plan on turning them off altogether. When you're in bed, the darker it is, the better you'll sleep. Even an illuminated alarm clock or telephone dial can be an annoyance when you're having trouble drifting off. If you want to be able to check the time during the night, opt for the kind of alarm clock that lights only when you press on it.

A Regular Routine

A few changes in your schedule can increase your chances of getting enough quality sleep to keep your stress in check and your happiness potential high. Even if your personality resists regular routines, your body likes them, so modifying your behaviour will cheer you up in the long run. It's a good idea to get up at around the same time each day (yes, even on weekends and vacations), to eat at more or less the same intervals, and to get to bed at around the same time each night, even if you don't feel especially sleepy when the hour arrives.

If you're worried about not being tired enough at bedtime, give serious thought to getting up about a half hour earlier than you have been. If it helps, you can adjust this in 10-minute increments during the course of a week or two. Getting up earlier will help you wind down earlier and it will expose you to more natural sunlight, which can improve your mood and help regulate your circadian rhythms.

Also, after you're awake, get up. There's an old joke that goes, *"If we were meant to pop out of bed in the morning we'd all sleep in toasters."* But lolling about between the sheets, unless perhaps for some active morning romance, is not conducive to falling back to sleep later on. (If you really need help getting up, consider getting a cat. As cat-lovers have pointed out, there's no such thing as a snooze alarm on a cat who wants breakfast.)

At first, altering your schedule might cause some mental stress or some social glitches, but your body will be grateful and will show its gratitude by sleeping long and well. This should more than compensate for any initial sense of inconvenience.

Bedtime Cooldowns

If you have difficulty going to sleep, getting ready for bed takes on a whole new meaning beyond brushing your teeth and putting on your pajamas. A little preplanned unwinding ritual or two can help get you in the right frame of mind to switch gears. Here are some things you can try:

- A warm bath. There was a reason your Mom gave you a bath before bedtime when you were small. It calms you down and signals that the energetic part of the day is done. Throw in a few drops of calming aromatherapy oil—a lavender fragrance is a wonderful choice—for extra help.

- Soft, soothing music. Music can help ease you toward sleep, and if you don't already have your own favourites there are a number of collections designed for this purpose. If you put the music on your smartphone, you can program it to turn off after a set number of minutes. Also consider trying "white noise" machines that re-create calming natural sounds such as waves or a forest rainfall.

- Sip some soothing tea. A number of herbal teas are said to have sleep-inducing properties. Experiment with valerian tea, chamomile, catnip, anise, or fennel tea. Most health-food stores also have special blends designed to help you slumber.

- Get some L-tryptophan. If you like milk, drinking a warm glass of it about a quarter of an hour before bedtime soothes the nervous system, thanks to its calcium and an amino acid called L-tryptophan. L-tryptophan is also found in turkey, chicken, cashews, beans, yogurt, and fresh cheeses such as ricotta, but keep your snacking small and light in the hours before bed.

- Gentle evening exercise. Doing 15 to 20 minutes of gentle exercise (yoga, t'ai chi, or walking) in the evening can provide your body with the oxygen it needs to sleep well. The trick is not to overdo it; stop exercising long enough before bedtime to allow your body to slow down. This slowdown period could take half an hour, but might take up to several hours. See what works best for you.

When it comes to bedtime cool downs, different solutions vary in their effectiveness for different people. You might have to play around to come up with one that works for you, but when you find one you like, you may well find it works consistently. Your brain will begin to associate your chosen technique with the onset of sleepiness.

Don't Just Lie There

If you're already in bed and feeling as if you have ants in your pants, is it time to count sheep? In a manner of speaking, yes. Counting sheep—or visualizing any benign, repetitive imagery (puppies, goldfish, or whatever you like) while counting—can make you pleasantly drowsy. If that doesn't do the trick, try one of these relaxation and visualization techniques:

- **Tummy circles.** Lie on your back and place your right palm on your navel, making tiny clockwise circles as you gently glide your hand. Let the circles gradually increase in size until they cover your stomach area. Then decrease the size of the circle again until you are right over your navel.

- **Toe twirls.** While lying on your back and keeping your feet still, turn your toes in a twirling motion—first clockwise, then counterclockwise, 10 times in each direction. Repeat. This simple exercise relaxes your entire body because, according to reflexologists, bodily energy channels called meridians converge there. Twirling the toes first stimulates then relaxes the meridians in your feet and, in so doing, relaxes every internal organ.

- **Progressive relaxation.** Close your eyes while lying on your back and begin to feel each part of your body in turn sinking into the mattress as it grows heavier and heavier. Begin with your feet, then follow in an upward-moving sequence with your ankles, calves, upper legs, abdomen, chest, arms, neck, jaw, eyes, and forehead—if you last that long!

- **Blow out the candles.** This sleep-inducer combines a calming visual stimulus with breath-based relaxation. Imagine a large round birthday cake with 100 glowing candles. Breathe in and think "100." Breathe out, as if blowing out a candle and think "99." Take another breath and repeat, counting backward until you count yourself among those who are happily sleeping.

- **Listen to your inner ocean.** As you lie on your back, place your hands behind your head with fingers— except thumbs—interlocked. Now use your thumbs to press gently on your lower earlobes so that they fold over the entrance to the ear canal. As you lie quietly, you will notice a deep, ocean-like sound inside your head. The sound will ebb and flow as you naturally breathe in and out. Simply focus on the noise—it's like creating your own personal "white noise" machine in your head.

- **Cast your eyes down.** A simple yoga technique for inducing sleep is to keep your eyes closed and aim them downward, as if you were looking down at the base of your nose. This signals the body that it's time to sleep. When eyes are focused straight ahead, the body is more alert.

- **Elevate your feet.** Take two pillows and place them under your feet. Yes, your feet. This posture signals your heart to slow down. It can also remind you of the way you feel when drifting off to sleep in a backyard hammock, swaying in the gentle breeze on a lazy afternoon.

- **Imagine a stormy day.** If you enjoy the feeling of *"stealing"* a few more minutes of slumber after you hit your snooze alarm on a workday morning, use this predilection to your advantage. Pretend it's your usual get-up time, but that you've just heard everything is closed due to an overnight storm. You've been given a reprieve to sleep in—enjoy it!

If you keep experimenting, you should be able to find a technique that works to help you get to sleep most nights. If there is a night when it is not working, try another. However, if there is an occasional night where nothing works and 30 minutes have passed, you will experience diminishing returns. Get up and pursue some quiet, non-stimulating activity such as inspirational reading (no news magazines or page-turning mysteries, please) or meditation. When you start to feel tired, go back to bed.

Happy Napping

If getting eight hours a night does not seem feasible for you, or even if it does, you might want to consider adding to your happiness potential by catching a nap. Scientists are discovering more and more evidence that a midday rest can improve mood; alertness; memory; and visual, motor, and spatial skills. As a study of 24,000 subjects showed, it can even improve cardiac health. Naps of 20 minutes are typically recommended if one is seeking these benefits.

But some researchers believe that even a five-minute midday nap can have a salutary effect. Although you might fear waking up groggy and inert after sleeping for such brief lengths of time, chances are you won't, because the short duration will prevent you from entering the deep state of sleep known as slow-wave sleep.

Many of us say we *"can't nap,"* but scientists would argue that we are naturally programmed to nap. So why have so many of us *"forgotten"* how to nap? One answer is that we've gotten out of the habit because our schedule is not conducive to napping. Another is that we live in a culture where napping can be considered morally suspect. Only the *"lazy"* and *"shiftless"* nap, we may tell ourselves.

With the stigma of napping rapidly becoming a thing of the past in our culture, it's a great time to give the practice a try. There is, however, one caveat. If you are seriously sleep-deprived, you might quickly fall into a deep sleep from which it is difficult to reorient. The power nap works best as a complement to adequate night-time slumber, not as compensation for chronic deprivation. The bottom line: to fulfil your happiness potential, it's best to get a good night's sleep and then some.

TWENTY

Health is Happiness

"Those who are nurtured best, survive best."

Louis Cozolino

How often have you heard someone say, *"If you have your health, you have everything"*? It might sound cliché, but as with many clichés, it is based on a universal truth. No matter how preoccupied we are with anything else in life, no matter how fulfilled we think we are, we quickly rearrange our priorities if we become unwell.

Health is happiness. That much we all agree on. But can happiness help us create, maintain, and restore good health?

Proactive Wellness

There are many definitions of health. The most basic definition is that it is the absence of disease. If we're not sick, we're healthy. Simple enough. But there are broader definitions that are not so cut-and-dry. Wellness of a somewhat more proactive sort can involve a conscious attempt to prevent illness. Someone can limit health risk factors by not smoking, not drinking too much alcohol, and not overeating.

But someone with a truly positive and proactive approach to wellness would be interested in more than fending off sickness. They would seek to optimize their health by doing such things as...

- Exercising regularly.

- Shopping for and preparing nutritious foods.

- Getting adequate sleep.

Beyond this, they would find ways to manage their negative stress, the effects of which can contribute to everything from coronary heart disease to diabetes to osteoporosis to irritable bowel syndrome, and on and on. To this end, they might engage in meditation, visualization, or other attention-focusing activities. Try to temper their hostilities and anxieties with humour, and take time to restore and renew their energies at regular intervals. Such a person would be taking a decisively salutary approach not only toward avoiding illness but also toward creating a state of maximum engagement in life and all it has to offer.

Wellness-Promoting Traits

It's long been known that negative emotions can undermine health. One well-known example involves the discovery of the correlation between heart disease and what has come to be known as *"Type A"* behaviour.

This connection gained widespread notoriety in the 1970s, thanks to the work of two San Francisco cardiologists, Meyer Friedman and Ray Rosenman, whose nine-year study of 3,000 men showed that those who were the most verbally hostile, the most easily angered, and the most impatient were also the most at risk not only for heart attacks but also for other forms of cardiovascular problems, including stroke.

Another link between negative emotions and poor health is that negative emotions are associated with adverse health behaviours. People with high levels of anger, depression, and anxiety are apt to smoke cigarettes, consume too much alcohol, avoid physical activity, and be overweight. But curbing negative emotions is not necessarily the same as proactively cultivating positive ones. (For example, it's one thing to be less hostile; it's another to deliberately cultivate a compassionate attitude.) Psychology wants to know if there are particular positive emotions that can engender optimum health. Two traits in particular are of special interest in this regard. The first is hope; the second—somewhat less predictably—is curiosity.

Hope and Health

Preliminary studies show a link between hope—which is essentially a manifestation of optimism and related positive points of view—and positive health outcomes. A hopeful orientation, it is believed, can heighten immune function and create resistance to illness. It can also motivate sensible behaviours with regard to personal health. Hopeful people tend to pay increased attention to health-relevant information, and optimistic beliefs are linked to greater processing of health-risk information.

There is, however, an important caveat when it comes to health and optimism. Individuals with an ideal level of optimism, the sort tempered by reason and logic, tend not to smoke, tend to use sunscreen, and tend to take vitamins and eat low-fat foods. Evidently, they are hopeful that both their preventive and proactive behaviours can raise the quantity and quality of their life span. On the other hand, individuals who see the future through glasses that are too rose-coloured overestimate their life span by as much as 20 years—and then, ironically, resist doing anything to make their wildly optimistic prophecy come true. In fact they behave in ways that are actually detrimental to their health and well-being.

No one is quite sure why some people are so optimistic that they become reckless. The reason might be purely—or at least partly—neurological. Rosy thoughts are triggered on a brain region called the rostral anterior cingulate cortex, an olive-sized cluster of neurons that activates when we think of hopes and aspirations or when we imagine happy events in the future. We may veer into irrational exuberance if this neural hub is too active, or perhaps we over activate this hub by wilfully denying reality. Either way the result is the same: cock-eyed optimism is detrimental to your health.

Curiosity and Self-Care

Curiosity may have killed the proverbial cat. But when it comes to humans, curiosity is another emotion that can have salutary health effects.

Scientific measures of curiosity measure the extent to which individuals in their usual environment are willing to explore novel stimuli. (For example: will a baby stop and stare at a new stuffed animal placed in its crib, or will the infant remain largely oblivious to the novel toy?) But basically, someone who is curious is someone who wants to learn, to investigate, and to incorporate new ideas and experiences. Presumably, some of the things they are likely to want to learn about and incorporate into their own lives are the latest developments in the areas of health and well-being. A curious person is far more likely than a blasé one to accumulate and draw on a rich store of health knowledge and resources.

Curiosity may also be linked to wellness because it constitutes a potential stress buffer. People who like to learn and who are able to sustain interest in engaging endeavours are the kinds of people who develop hobbies and pursue *"flow"* activities. Their periods of heightened focus and attentiveness serve to divert their minds from worry.

Changing Negative Health Habits

Even negative habits serve certain purposes that, in themselves, might not be bad. Someone might smoke to relieve feelings of stress. Someone might become a workaholic to ease a sense of loneliness. If such habits are terminated without anything to put in their place, the underlying emotions could wreak havoc. However, if the smoker substitutes deep breathing exercise for lighting up, or the workaholic finds an active social organization that will lure him out of the office, they stand a better chance of successfully disrupting their self-destructive patterns.

Researchers who study motivation and goal attainment also note that it is easier to achieve a very specific goal than it is to achieve a vague or general one. Those who wish to change a habit are better off vowing, for example, to exercise on a treadmill or bicycle for 30 minutes a day than to simply *"get in shape this year."* Positive social support is also exceedingly helpful when it comes to changing a habit. Merely announcing your intentions to people who will encourage you can serve as a motivator because your commitment to change is now a *"matter of record"* rather than a silent wish. And should you be tempted to backslide, your supporters can remind you of your good intentions, buck up your spirits, or simply commiserate compassionately and offer you shoulders on which to cry.

Changing a habit is never easy. It involves being patient with oneself, being tolerant of frustration, being curious about what life afterward will be like, and being hopeful that things will be better. If one relies on friends and loved ones to help, then it also involves trusting them. The more one can employ their strengths in the service of change, the likelier that change is to occur.

Hardiness, Resilience, and Recovery

Of course even the happiest and most optimistic people sometimes succumb to illness. The psychology of happiness is also interested in the role of positive emotions and attitudes in helping people recover from illness or, where recovery is not possible, to cope well with the effects of illness. The idea that certain positive emotions could aid recovery from sickness took hold in the popular imagination in 1979 when Norman Cousins, a high-profile magazine editor, published a best-selling book entitled Anatomy of an Illness. The book recounted Cousins' recovery from a debilitating collagen disease. Cousins attributed his cure, in large part, to his decision to check out of a hospital and into a hotel, where he spent his days laughing uproariously at old Marx Brothers movies he'd rented as *"therapy."* Though there was some scepticism about the efficacy of his method (some said he'd have recovered anyway, and some said he owed more to getting out of a negative hospital environment than to his laugh treatment per se), Cousins' book became a potent catalyst for scientific investigations into the healing power of humour and other positive emotions.

Those sorts of investigations are ongoing. Scientists are attempting to supplement abundant anecdotal evidence with hard empirical data linking recovery from various health conditions to patient's moods, attitudes, and self-directed behaviours. And many researchers believe we are on the threshold of a new understanding of what is being called *"the biology of hope."*

Hardiness is the ability to discern meaning in life and to rise to challenges in spite of taxing demands and hardships. Still, no one would deny that there are infirmities and illnesses the effects of which are enduring. Psychologists are also interested in how and why certain people in the grips of chronic illnesses or permanent disabilities still manage to thrive. (Think about Christopher Reeves, for example, who inspired millions after his spinal cord injury.) Why do some physically challenged people still exhibit so much hardiness?

Although some people who are beset with illness and afflictions give in to depression and despair, others do not. The latter group...

- Manages to maintain a coherent view of their life, integrating all realities-even seemingly illogical and unpleasant ones.

- Does not dwell on the unfairness or randomness of their ailments.

- Is open to learning valuable lessons from the experience they've been dealt.

An individual who is determined to remain positive in the face of negative health developments does not bemoan their fate and ask the universe, *"Why me?"* Rather they ask, *"Why not me? What does this challenge have to offer me?"* Their attitude keeps them engaged in seeking out life's opportunities. Psychology would say that such individuals refuse to participate in the pathogenic model of illness, which sees disease as an enemy. By focusing on what one can still accomplish and relish even in the face of illness, they are pursuing a salutogenic model. They look for what's right with them, rather than what's wrong with them. This does not mean they deny their illness (indeed, they will do whatever is necessary to instigate improvement) but rather that they adapt to it and manage it. The salutogenic patient refuses to feel helpless.

Researchers who focus on salutogenic individuals and their creative and adaptive strategies for dealing with ailments and afflictions often cite Beethoven as an example of a remarkable individual who lived fully and functioned with an exceptional level of creativity despite physiological limitations. The composer conveyed stirring beauty through his music despite the deafness imposed upon him. Individuals with salutogenic perspectives abound today as well—from renowned celebrities such as physicist Stephen Hawking to athletic competitors in the Paralympics' games of wheelchair tennis, archery, and rugby.

Researcher Aaron Antonovsky, a professor in the Sociology of Health department at Israel's Ben Gurion University of

Negev, has noted that those who thrive despite ailments and injuries actually manifest an opposite reaction to stressful life events. Although the average person views sudden life changes and daily hassles as negative stressors, salutogenic thrivers see them as a means of becoming mentally and emotionally stronger.

CHAPTER 6
FINAL WORDS

Nowadays people in the developed world are, on the whole, living longer than ever before. That longevity stems, at least in part, from advances in health care as well as in sanitation and nutrition. Still, some people live longer than others while some age with a greater sense of contentment and engagement than others, making their elderly years rewarding.

Do the Happy Live Longer?

Will we have more years if the years we do have are filled with positive emotion? If so, that certainly seems like a win-win situation. Happily, the answer appears to be yes. Research has found strong associations between positive emotional experiences and longevity.

Should additional studies continue to point to causality between long life and positive emotion, scientists will be searching in earnest for reasons why positive emotions lead to longevity. Some possible explanations are that positive people are more likely to...

- Promote their own health by eating well and exercising.

- Seek and benefit from the health-promoting effects of social support.

- Be married or in de facto (married or in a stable relationship people, in general, live longer than single people).

- Engage in altruistic activities (do-gooders appear to be healthier for the doing).

- Use humour as a coping strategy (laughter boosts immunity).

- Deal with stress (and so avoid many of stress' illness-inducing effects).

There might even turn out to be underlying biological differences between optimists and pessimists, themselves tied to a more robust constitution. But whatever the explanation, if positive attitudes do indeed turn out to be a ticket to a longer life, two things are true: positive mind set people will have more time in which to be upbeat. And pessimists who obsessively worry about the future may not have as long a future to worry about.

Happiness and the Life Cycle

The study of happiness and aging has led to another intriguing finding. Even those of us who are fundamentally happy, it turns out, experience varying degrees of happiness depending on what phase of life we are in. The average person will have predefined periods in their life in which they will be happier than others.

The U-Shaped Curve of Happiness

A recent study of the U.S. population showed that happiness follows what is called a *"U-shaped"* curve. It starts out strong, but then declines steadily between the ages of 16 and 45. Then it starts to swing upward again, and rises for 15 years. (Interestingly, the 15-year upswing in happiness that follows age 45 is stronger than the upswing that tracks doubling of income. The trend appears to be age-related rather than related to having more disposable funds or a larger nest egg.)

The U-shaped happiness pattern is not a totally new finding. However, in the past, researchers couldn't tell whether 55-year-olds were happier than 45-year-olds in a given year because the 55-year-olds had aged or because of what is known as the cohort effect. Maybe the older people were born to a more upbeat generation or were part of a generation that experienced less hardship throughout their lives. The recent study gets around this problem by combining data on people of different ages at different points in time over the course of a quarter-century. The authors were able to compare not only 55- and 45-year-olds today, but also people who are 55-year-olds today to people who were 55 a decade ago. Even when they accounted for when people were born, the U-shaped happiness pattern remained. This appears to indicate that age itself has a definite impact on happiness.

The Happiness Mid-Life Crisis

So why does happiness start out strong, dip in middle age, and then revive among the elderly? This is another happiness puzzle that requires further exploration.

The authors of the recent study, David Blanchflower and Andrew Oswald, are economists rather than psychologists, but they note that the pattern of happiness does not match the usual pattern of wealth accrual. Wealth tends to rise steadily during the life cycle, peaking around retirement age, but happiness doesn't follow the same trajectory. Once again it appears that money cannot actually buy happiness.

Blanchflower and Oswald speculate that people in mid-life experience unhappiness because they *"quell the infeasible aspirations of their youth."* In other words, they give up on some of their youthful dreams. But this still does not explain the upswing in happiness that occurs after one's mid-40s.

That, it turns out, could well have something to do with another quality that tends to increase as we age: wisdom.

A Wealth of Wisdom

The psychoanalyst Erik H. Erikson, well known for his theory on personality development from birth through old age, linked each stage of life with an either/or proposition. Our latter years, he said, are characterized by either a path toward despair or a path toward ego integrity. He also linked each stage with a virtue. The virtue of our elder years, Erikson said, was wisdom. It was wisdom that could help us avoid despair and experience a satisfying, meaningful conclusion to our lives.

However, when it came to defining, what exactly, the virtue of wisdom comprised, Erikson was less than precise. His vagueness left psychologists with open questions. As of late, more and more of them are seeking answers.

Older and Wiser

The quality we call wisdom is something many people feel they simply recognize when they encounter it. And indeed our associations with it often seem to involve images of the elderly. When we imagine someone going off to see the tribal wise-man or wise woman we picture them sitting at the feet of a thoughtful, twinkle-eyed, gray-haired sage—not consulting a lanky adolescent. When we think of one of the Waltons—the beloved TV family—needing definitive advice from a family member, we know that it was Grandma or

Grandpa Walton, not John Boy, who helped them resolve their dilemma. Wisdom, as those who are now studying it agree, is not necessarily a product of advanced age, but being older increases the chances of accruing the variety of life experiences and the maturity that generate the quality. Still, positive psychologists, gerontological psychologists, and even neuroscientists armed with brain-scanning equipment want to know more about how to identify and quantify wisdom. Some who are studying this virtue believe that doing so is essential to our future as individuals and as a society.

Wise Ways

Although defining wisdom presents a challenge, consistent pieces of the definition are appearing. Certain aspects of wisdom show up over and over in the growing body of literature on this topic. Elements of the evolving definition include the following:

- The ability to learn from experience. Wise people may not get things right the first time, or even the second, but at a certain point the light dawns and they change behaviour that isn't serving them. Unlike those whom wisdom eludes, they don't act like mice traversing the same maze paths over and over when there's no tidbit of cheese to be found at the end.

- Flexibility. The wise are not rigidly wed to one way of doing things. They are always open to new information and new possibilities. They understand that life includes a certain amount of uncertainty, even randomness, and they are able to modify their plans accordingly.

- Effective coping with adversity. When things don't work out well, the wise don't fall apart. They are calm in the face of crisis. They adapt to misfortune in ways that can help them continue to thrive—even against the odds. After a crisis is past, they know how to rebound and move on.

- Objectivity. The wise can view situations with a certain level of healthy detachment. They try not to let personal biases determine their decisions or course of action. They lack prejudice, or at least police themselves to detect any vestiges of it.

- Careful deliberation. The wise look before they leap. They resist impulsivity and are unlikely to jump to conclusions without considering all available evidence. They ask good questions of others and of themselves.

- Balance. Wise people draw on both their logic and their well-honed emotional intelligence when making decisions.

- A lack of self-absorption. Wise people tend to be *"other centred."* They are unselfish. They exude empathy and compassion.

- Humility. Though they may be exemplary individuals, the wise are not stuck-up about it. They never assume they are infallible. As Gandhi—who often tops the list when people are asked to name a wise role model— put it, *"It is unwise to be too sure of one's wisdom."*

Emotional Regulation

Within the emotional component of wisdom is what researchers consider to be an especially important ability common to people who exemplify this virtue. That quality is known as emotional regulation, or the ability to maintain emotional equilibrium during a wide variety of positive and negative circumstances.

There is a well-known analogy in psychology that compares humans' reaction to emotion to an image of a horse and a rider. We can either treat our emotions as a horse, with ourselves as the rider, or treat our emotions as the rider and ourselves as the horse. In other words, we can tame our emotions or let them run away with us. Wise people do the former.

Neuroscientists at the University of Wisconsin have been examining patterns of brain activity associated with emotional regulation in a group of older adults (the average age is 64). In a paper published in 2006, the team reported that the individuals in the group who regulated their emotions well (the riders) showed a distinctly different pattern of brain activity than those who did not (the horses). The former group evidently used their prefrontal cortex, the part of the brain that exerts "executive control" over certain brain functions, to moderate activity in the amygdala, the small interior brain region that processes fear, anger, and anxiety. In the latter group, activity in the amygdala was higher.

In addition, daily measurements of the stress hormone cortisol showed that it, too, was elevated in the *"rider"* group. The combination of high amygdala activity and high cortisol often results in poor health outcomes. Wisconsin researcher Richard Davidson, noted that the subjects with lower amygdala activity were skilled at regulating negative emotion and voluntarily using their thought processes to reappraise situations. Although they registered the negative, they had somehow learned not to let it overwhelm them. Davidson added that these kinds of capabilities probably result from *"something that has been at least implicitly trained over the years."*

Leaving a Positive Legacy

Another element that can factor in to late-life hardiness and happiness is continuing to feel that what one does is of consequence. As it turns out, many feel that the products of their actions in their latter years are of special significance.

Leaving a legacy is linked with living a life of meaning and purpose. Not surprisingly, older individuals who have been actively engaged with leaving a positive footprint on the world and are satisfied that they will be well-remembered are likely to face their final years with a sense of satisfaction—the satisfaction that comes from a job well done.

Leaving something that lives beyond us is a goal that can be approached in many ways. Writing a will is the classic way we pass on material things. One can leave a legacy of wealth to be used for all manner of good causes—donations to charity, scholarship endowments, or sending one's own grandkids to medical school. But money is by no means the only meaningful thing we can leave behind.

We can leave the fruits of artistic endeavours—memoirs, stories, and poems we've written; artworks and crafts we've created; music we've made; we've taken; sweaters we've knitted.

We can leave the fruits of our knowledge—the advice we've given, the effects of decisions we've made and helped others to make.

We can leave a business. We can leave an invention. We can leave a mathematical formula or a scientific theory, or a psychological construct.

But even if we leave none of those things, we can leave the impression we have made on those we've known. We can leave a legacy of kindness, of laughter, and of love. Even with the bulk of our life behind us, we can still keep working on our legacy. And if we believe that what survives us brings others joy, even in some small way, we can be happy about that.

Live Long and Prosper

For anyone interested in unlocking the secrets of happiness, this is an exciting time. Never before have so many fine minds and so many resources been devoted to such a life-affirming subject.

But no matter how much we as a society learn about happiness, each of us as individuals must create our recipe for a happy life. As with all good recipes, there can be many variations on a theme. But don't forget the basic ingredients: Look on the bright side. Being optimistic is no guarantee that things will turn out as you wish. But it certainly doesn't prevent them from turning out that way, and may help you create the circumstances you seek. Much more importantly, however, optimism will enable you to weather life's storms with greater equanimity by understanding that there is often an upside to a downturn that will reveal itself in time.

Be true to yourself. Stand up for what you think is right and do what is right for you. Don't feel you must always conform, or you will doom yourself to an unsatisfying and endless trek on the social treadmill.

Be kind. Kindness, love, and compassion breed more of the same. In the end, your relationships with those close to you and with the world at large are a mirror of how you conduct yourself.

Be generous. Share your time and your talents with others. Giving to others not only helps them but also benefits you. The feedback loop of giving is an infinite pathway to happiness: do good, feel good. Feel good, do good.

Play with a passion. Indulge in your favourite pursuits whenever you can. Use, improve, and build on your skills in those activities. Get involved enough so that *"time flies."* Try to spend at least some of your work time employing your strengths and skills. The more you can do this, the more work will feel like play.

Try new things. Curiosity is curative. Always remain open to learning. Allow yourself to take some risks and stretch your comfort zone. There is nothing like the thrill of a new challenge to make you feel joyfully alive.

Look on the light side. Humour is a tonic that will perk up your energy and bolster your spirits. It will help you keep things in perspective and even rebound from crises. And there is nothing like sharing a laugh to help you bond with others.

Explore your spiritual beliefs. Even if you have no formal religious affiliation, contemplate on your soulful aspects. Recognize those moments when you feel connected to something larger than yourself. Doing so can infuse your life with a profound sense of meaning.

Seek out positive people. Relationships can be great sources of happiness if the relationships you have involve reciprocal trust and respect. Seek out people whose company is enjoyable and uplifting, and who make you feel confident in yourself rather than dependent on them. Last but not least, spend time with people who are fun!

Take good care of yourself. Exercise, eat well, and make sure you get enough sleep. Try to spend some time each day in a quiet, restorative activity such as meditation. Your body needs the right fuel to maintain a long, healthy, happy life.

Express your thankfulness. Be actively grateful for the good things in your life. Tally them up, write them down. Express your thanks directly to people who have helped or inspired you. The more you look for things to be grateful for, the more of them you will find.

Finally, discover and fulfil your purpose. Have a reason to be excited about the future and your contribution to it. Set goals throughout the whole of your life and, as you reach them, set others—even until the end. One day your life, no matter how long, will be someone else's memory. Make it a happy memory.

Bibliography

Allport, G. (1950). *The Individual and His Religion.*

Clampitt, Phillip, DeKoch, & Robert Transforming. (2010). *Leaders Into Progress Makers.*

Csikszentmihalyi, M. (1998). *Finding Flow: The Psychology of Engagement With Everyday Life. Basic Books.* . ISBN 0-465-02411-4 .

Csikszentmihalyi, M., & Nakamura, J. (2011). Positive psychology: Where did it come from, where is it going? In T. B. K.M. Sheldon, *Designing positive psychology* (pp. 2-9). New York, NY: Oxford University Press.

Diener, E. (1984). Subjective well-being. *Psychol Bull,* 95:542–575.

Diener, E., & Biswas-Diener, R. (2002). Will money increase subjective well-being? *Soc Indic Res.,* 57:119–169.

Diener, E., & Suh, E. (1999). Well-Being: The Foundations of Hedonic Psychology. In D. E. Kahneman D. New York: Russell Sage Foundation;.

Fredrickson, B. (2009). *Positivity.* New York: Crown.

Fredrickson, B. (2013). *Love 2.0.* New York: Hudson Street Press.

Fredrickson, B. L. (2013). Positive emotions broaden and build. In E. Ashby Plant, & P. G. Devine, *Advances on*

Experimental Social Psychology, 47 (pp. 1-53). Burlington: Academic Press.

Fredrickson, B. L. (2013). Updated thinking on the positivity ratio. In *American Psychologist, 68* (pp. 814-822).

Goleman, D. (1995). *Emotional intelligence.* New York: Bantam.

Goleman, D. (1998). *Working with emotional intelligence.* New York: Bantam/ Doubleday/Dell.

Kahneman, D., & Riis, J. (2005). The Science Of Well-Being. In B. N. Huppert FA. Oxford: Oxford Univ. Press.

Pausch, R. (n.d.). University Lecture Series: Journeys. In P. 15213. United States: Carnegie Mellon University.

Peterson, C., & Seligman, M. E. (2004). *Character strengths and virtues: A handbook and classification.* Oxford: Oxford University Press. ISBN 0-19-516701-5.

Peterson, C., Maier, S. F., & Seligman, M. E. (1996). *Learned Helplessness.* ISBN: 9780195044676.

Seligman, M. E. (1991). *Learned Optimism: How to Change Your Mind and Your Life.* New York, NY: Pocket Books.

Seligman, M. E. (2002). *Authentic Happiness: Using the New Positive Psychology to Realize Your Potential for Lasting Fulfillment.* New York, NY: Free Press.

Seligman, M. E. (2004). *Can Happiness be Taught?* Daedalus, Spring.

Singer, P. (2015). *The Most Good You Can Do: How Effective Altruism Is Changing Ideas About Living Ethically.* Yale University Press.

Stutzer, A., Bruno, & Frey. (2008). Stress that Doesn't Pay. In S. J., *Economics 110(2)* (pp. 339–366, 2008 DOI: 10.1111/j.1467-9442.2008.00542.x).

www.ingramcontent.com/pod-product-compliance
Lightning Source LLC
Chambersburg PA
CBHW051817090426
42736CB00011B/1532